Siwa

Siwa

Jewelry, Costume, and
Life in an Egyptian Oasis

Margaret Vale

The American University in Cairo Press
Cairo New York

All images are by Margaret Vale except when otherwise indicated.

This edition published in 2014 by
The American University in Cairo Press
113 Sharia Kasr el Aini, Cairo, Egypt
420 Fifth Avenue, New York, NY 10018
www.aucpress.com

Exclusive distribution outside Egypt and North America by I.B.Tauris & Co Ltd., 6 Salem Road, London, W2 4BU

Dar el Kutub No. 10468/14
ISBN 978 977 416 681 5

Dar el Kutub Cataloging-in-Publication Data
Vale, Margaret
Siwa: Jewelry, Costume, and Life in an Egyptian Oasis / Margaret Vale.—Cairo: The American University in Cairo Press, 2014
        p. : ill. ; cm.
        ISBN: 978 977 416 681 5
                1. Siwah oasis (Egypt)
                I. Title
                916.21

1 2 3 4 5   18 17 16 15 14

Designed by Sally Boylan
Printed in Egypt

For my family
And in memory of my beloved parents and brother

Contents

Acknowledgments

I have many people to thank for their help in writing this book, which came about through several years of visiting Siwa. My thanks go first and foremost to Asmaa who generously shared her knowledge of the Oasis. She also gave me friendship and wonderful hospitality. Ahmed Ali Heda taught me about Siwa and its history, and Mahdi Huweiti gave me constant help, patient support, and encouragement. Senoussi Abdallah Abdel-Magid, and his mother—granddaughter of the silversmith Senoussi Daddoum Aani (Gab Gab)—were always helpful, and enthusiastic about the project. I thank them all for their patience because this book was a long time in the making. I also very much appreciated the help, and the warm and generous hospitality given me by their families. I cannot thank them enough.

I also want to express my thanks to Abu Bakr Ismail, curator of the Siwa House Museum, and Hassan Muhammad Ahmed Jerry, who was then working there. I appreciated being allowed to photograph artefacts, and learn about them in such a welcoming and delightful environment. I owe a debt of gratitude to many people in Siwa who helped me in one way or another and I thank Dr. Abd El-Aziz Aldumairy, Abdallah Abu Bakr Twati, Muhammad Ibrahim Eissa, Abdallah Baghi, Muhammad Ibrahim Moussa, Muhammad Moussa, and Muhammad Zeit. Hadi Muhammad Hameyid and Hajj Mustapha, Mansour A. Gomaa, and Saleh Ibrahim Abdel-Salam gave me useful ideas during informal conversations. I also want to thank the two young Siwan women working for the Siwa and Tangier Project at the Siwa House Museum for the help they gave me.

In Alexandria I was so grateful to a neighbor of the silversmith Master Amin, who left his office to translate for me. In Kerdassa, Muhammad Said Eissa kindly showed me around his family's weaving workshop and introduced me to the weavers. In his shop, Mustapha Hudeib kindly answered my questions about the *tarfutet*.

I am most grateful to Mariam Rosser-Owen and Marianne Ellis at the Victoria and Albert Museum—Marianne Ellis kindly examined items of Siwan dress to tell me the names of the stitches that had been used. Thanks are due to Julie Hudson at the British Museum, and Amelia Maclellan and Kathie Way at the Natural History Museum in London. I also thank weaver Bobbie Kociejowski, Victoria Connolly, and Valerie Barkowski, who in separate conversations, gave me invaluable suggestions. I thank the reviewers for the American University in Cairo for their useful comments on a copy of the manuscript in 2006.

In the Anthropology Library of the British Museum the staff was of great help. I would also like to thank staff at the Royal Geographical Society for all their assistance; Joy Wheeler, of the Image Department, kindly responded to my requests for pictures

As I have been writing this book, friends and family have encouraged me, offered support, and made useful suggestions, and I particularly want to thank my friend Dr. Leila Chakravarti. My brother John, who did the skilful drawings, was always patient and understanding. And thanks are due to my husband Brian, for his help and support.

My deepest gratitude goes to the Siwan women who befriended me. I cannot thank them enough; they introduced me to their crafts, customs, and ceremonies, and showed me hospitality, generosity, and tolerance. I hope they will feel I did their handicrafts justice, and will excuse any inadequacies.

In the text, pseudonyms are used for women because of their protected status in the oasis, and for men when only a first name is given.

Introduction

S iwa is an isolated oasis in the heart of the Western Desert of Egypt, close to the Libyan border. It is a place of great natural beauty set among palm and olive groves, and inhabited by a people of Berber origin. My interest in Siwa began in the 1980s. At that time, the oasis was distant and inaccessible, cut off without rail or road links to the outside world. Historically, its connections with other places had been through camel caravans, seasonal labor migration, and its position on the annual pilgrimage route from the Maghreb to the Red Sea and thence to Mecca, but, in the mid-1980s, things were changing: electricity and television had already arrived, and a tarmac road from the coast was completed. My first visit to Siwa took place with a group of friends within months of the road opening, after we had obtained written permission from the authorities. It was only after hours of driving through empty desert on a long straight road that we caught our first glimpse of its date groves and olive trees, its springs and salt lakes, and its spectacular mud walls, towers, and houses.

It was inevitable that improved access by road would precipitate a radical change in a lifestyle that had developed for centuries in semi-isolation. And when, in 1999, I returned for a stay of three months, the first of six visits (between 1999 and 2013), it was clear that this expectation was being fulfilled. Siwans were beginning to enjoy the new benefits of more modern forms of housing; jobs in tourism, hotels, shops, and government offices; income from the sale of their crafts to tourists; and the promise of an easier life. But there were concerns that their community was losing its unique character, customs, and values. There was a feeling of optimism for the future, but at the same time nostalgia for the Siwa of the past. People were beginning to wonder what the future would bring for their children. Conservationists were also worried by the construction of cement buildings, for it is the traditional mud architecture as well as the antiquities, the springs, the palm gardens, the lakes, and the surrounding desert landscape that give the place its character. There was even a fear that some of the palm or olive gardens might be cleared for development.

Tourism had begun to transform the Siwans' colorful and distinctive crafts: pottery, baskets, silver jewelry, and embroidery had been produced for their own use for generations. The most significant—not to say famous—traditional feature of Siwa was the unique style of its silver jewelry. Developed over centuries of semi-isolation, its main attributes are a pendant disc which can reach the size of a saucer; a torque; long chains that fall from necklaces and head ornaments; bosses; and plaques engraved with astral, floral, and vegetal patterns.

My interest in Middle Eastern jewelry began in 1975 when my family and I went to live in the Saudi Arabian capital of Riyadh. The price of oil had gone up by four hundred percent only the year before, and the kingdom suddenly found itself rich. The traditional nature of Saudi society soon ensured that money percolated down into every nook and cranny, causing dramatic changes in the lives of the people. The desert Bedouin were probably affected the most, many exchanging their nomadic existence for a settled lifestyle and moving from black tents to houses built of clay bricks or cinder block. Some moved into towns and cities where they could earn a regular wage or drive taxis. Others worked for the oil companies, sending money back to their families, who were sometimes still living in tents, to pay for unprecedented luxuries such as refrigerators, stoves, and pick-up trucks. Mass-produced goods began to flood in from overseas, displacing the traditional products of local silversmiths, metal workers, weavers, and potters. And the souqs in the towns and cities were soon brimming with glittering machine-made gold and other fashionable items.

Foreigners in Riyadh were, however, still enthralled by the traditional crafts of the kingdom, especially the spectacular silver and base-metal jewelry. Visiting the corner of the souq in Riyadh where jewelry and fabrics were sold and meeting with the veiled women merchants who were selling embroidered Bedouin dresses and silver ornaments from metal bowls was always an enjoyable experience. That said, it was also somewhat frustrating because, in addition to its visual appeal, it was clear that the jewelry and embroideries contained intriguing forms and motifs whose meaning could only be discovered by understanding more about the social backgrounds and traditions of the women who wore them. Although I had a particular rapport with two of the women and learned as much as I could about the jewelry, I did not have the opportunity to look into it any further.

In the 1980s, I was able to continue my interest in traditional crafts when I spent four years in Egypt. The Souq al-Sagha of Cairo and the Souq al-Attarine in Alexandria were filled with old as well as newly crafted jewelry, and beautiful silver items from the oasis of Siwa could occasionally be found. These were what first aroused my interest in this remote and fascinating place. I learned more from Ahmed Fakhry's 1973 book *The Oases of Egypt*, and from local writers, especially Susan Weeks, whose regular articles and drawings of the silver jewelry of the Bedouin of the Western Desert and the settled peoples of the oases were published in *Cairo Today*, a weekly magazine. I visited Cairo's museums and regular craft shops, like the folklorist Shahira Mehrez's shop in Dokki and Leila and Omar Rachad's downtown shop where examples of Siwan costume and jewelry, embroidery, baskets, and pottery were displayed, and hoped that someday I would be able to travel to see this mysterious place for myself.

Jewelry had always been important to Siwan women; in part because it embellished the body and enhanced their good looks, and also because it was intrinsically valuable. But beside these attributes, jewelry performed other functions for the wearer. Its spiritually protective function was the most important, especially for people living in an isolated environment without the benefits of modern medicine or electricity, and surrounded by mysterious pharaonic tombs, dark caves, narrow passages, underground tunnels, and deep glittering springs.

Traditionally, the jewelry was manufactured from silver coins sent by customers to be melted down in the crucible of local silversmiths, such as Senoussi Daddoum Aani (who died in 1958 and was known as Gab Gab), whose work before the 1940s is legendary in the oasis. From the middle of the twentieth century, however, the preference of Siwan women for distinctive handcrafted silver jewelry began to give way in favor of machine-made gold that increased exposure to the outside world had convinced them was fashionable. But some pieces continued to be worn by the women to festivals with their ceremonial (wedding) costume. Some of the elderly women wear certain silver pieces daily, and silver still has a resonance in the oasis.

Jewelry was my main focus, but I also became interested in the embroidery and elaboration of traditional Siwan wedding clothes. On many cool winter afternoons in the oasis, Siwan friends introduced me to their embroidery designs and stitches. Using silky thread in the traditional colors of red, yellow, orange, green, and black, I learned to stitch the tiny motifs that depict the familiar objects and landscapes that surround them, and which belong to a local artistic vocabulary that extends across their craft to the skill of painting the skin with henna.

This book seeks to record something of the fascination and allure of the traditional jewelry, costume, and crafts of the men and women of Siwa against a background of the history, customs, and ceremonies in which they are rooted. It is also concerned with daily life in the oasis, and how the women have responded to the modern world—the impact of drastic change on their lives and on their taste in clothes and adornment.

1 North African Jewelry and Textiles

The silver ornaments and embroidered, hand-woven garments that comprise the traditional dress of Siwa Oasis exemplify the variety of jewelry and textile traditions found across North Africa. This is a broad region that extends from the Mediterranean Sea to the desert vastness of the Sahara, and from the Gulf of Suez in the east to the rugged mountains and Atlantic coast of Morocco in the west. With the exception of the green and fertile valley of the Nile, the landscape of the interior is of arid desert with a scatter of oases, agricultural settlements, and sand-colored towns and cities.

This apparently unpromising area has been nevertheless a vibrant historical crossroads for peoples and civilizations. Originally the home of indigenous Berbers, Egyptians, Nubians, and Sudanese, North Africa has been subsequently fought over and successively colonized by Phoenicians, Greeks, Romans, Vandals, Byzantines, Arabs, and Ottoman Turks. Each successively introduced their religions, cultural traditions, and artistic techniques and designs. The region was also linked to the four points of the compass by trade routes, both by water and by land. Gold, ivory, and slaves came overland or along the Nile from south of the Sahara; tin, copper, and amber from Europe, beyond Gibraltar and the Pillars of Hercules; and precious fabrics, jewels, and spices along the Silk Road which led from China.

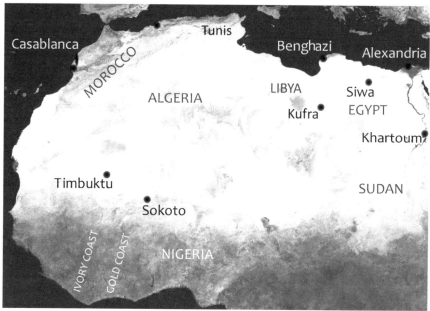

1. North Africa and the Sahara. *NASA.*

Jewelry

Traces of Roman and Byzantine influences can still be found in North African jewelry, but the most significant, unifying, and lasting cultural impact was made by the Islamic Arab invasions of the seventh century. The arts flowered under the patronage of the various kingdoms and caliphates that ruled in the region until the fifteenth century: the Umayyads in Damascus, the Abbasids in Baghdad, the Fatimids in North Africa and then in Egypt, and the Berber dynasties of Morocco— the Almoravids followed by the Almohads—who ruled in North Africa and Spain.

Metalworking, in particular, reached an advanced stage in terms of technique and design, and received an infusion of new ideas and skills with the arrival of Jewish and Muslim silversmiths and goldsmiths expelled by the Catholic monarchs of Spain following the Christian conquest of Granada in 1492. Metalworkers became important members of the community as the production of jewelry involved the transformation of metal by fire, and its forging and manipulation seemed to signify special powers that gave the craft an aura of magic, danger, and mystery. The general population found this disturbing, and metalworkers therefore formed a group apart, hence the defensive sickle symbol used by Berber metalsmiths.

Gold *(dahab)*, the most highly prized of precious metals, was worn in cities, but in the rural areas silver *(fada)*, prized for a white, luminous sheen that was reminiscent of the moon, was the metal of choice. Across the Middle East and North Africa, a type of personal jewelry evolved that was impressively bold and decorative. Indeed, until comparatively recently, Bedouin, oasis dwellers, and villagers still wore an abundance of silver ornaments. Some pieces incorporated amber, copal resin, carnelian, coral, and amazonite, or more affordable materials like glass and shell. Jewelry adorned the head, was displayed around the shoulders and breast, and encircled arms and ankles. A woman would acquire a large collection of ornaments over her lifetime, starting with the items that comprised her *mahr*, that is the bridewealth. These would be worn and flaunted at ceremonial gatherings and festivals.

Textiles

Jewelry placed in burials or hidden in the ground in times of political unrest has survived and left a record of the evolution of styles and techniques, but cloth soon deteriorates and little is known about North African textiles from ancient times. Egypt's dry climate, however, preserved items of clothing from royal tombs of the New Kingdom that are decorated with pattern-weaving and some of the earliest examples of embroidery. Quantities of fragments of cloth and a few garments were found in burials, and in the ancient rubbish mounds of Fustat, the first Arab settlement in Egypt that is now a part of Cairo. Influenced by Greek and Byzantine sources, they are colorful with characteristic bands and roundels enclosing figurative depictions of animals, birds, and people. The typical garment is a T-shaped linen or woolen tunic, sometimes decorated from shoulder to hem or waist with a woven or embroidered band. Garments of this shape were worn for centuries and echoes of it can be seen today in North Africa.

The early Islamic dynasties, the Umayyads and Abbasids, brought cultural change and innovation. Figural images continued to be depicted on textiles, metalwork, and other objects for domestic or personal use, but urban Muslims began to favor a sort of continuous vine pattern called arabesque, geometric designs, and calligraphy. These became common designs for Islamic ornament used to decorate walls, woodwork, metal, and cloth alike.

From the eighth to the twelfth centuries, embroidered or woven inscriptions, called *tiraz*, were a common form of textile decoration. Initially made in royal workshops for the use of the ruler, *tiraz* bands were later produced in public workshops and factories. Given the name *tiraz al-'amm*, they made fine materials and woven and embroidered bands with inscriptions such as "In the Name of God," "Good fortune," and "Prosperity." These *tiraz* workshops flourished in the Maghreb, especially in Fez in Morocco; in Egypt, in Alexandria, Cairo, Akhmim, and Bahnasa; and in Spain. Inscribed bands, woven or embroidered with silks on cotton or linen, were used to embellish turbans and veils and the neck and sleeves of tunics of the rich. By the late Fatimid period in Egypt, the end of the twelfth century, inscriptions were sometimes replaced with patterns that imitated the forms of calligraphy, or with small medallions enclosing birds, fish, and animals. Embroidery was popular with the Mamluks who followed the Fatimids, for the decoration of tunics, belts, the lower edges of trouser legs, hats, shoes, and sleeve handkerchiefs. Fragments of embroidered tunic fronts with stand-up collars that survived from the Mamluk period belonged to a form of garment which was probably the forerunner of today's *gallabiya*.[1]

In the sixteenth century, Ottoman expansion in North Africa brought well-documented Turkish influences to urban fashions together with new techniques and designs in the weaving of cloth and embroidery.

Influences

The impact of Islamic styles on the design and manufacture of jewelry and textiles in North Africa was nevertheless moderated by the resilience of an indigenous population that was rural and conservative, and already had strong artistic traditions. The most significant of these were the Berbers, who inhabited an extensive area stretching from the Atlantic to the oasis of Siwa, inside the Egyptian border. During the Arab invasions the Berbers were forced to withdraw to the mountains and remote desert regions where they still live. They continued to use geometric patterns such as the cross, diamond, circle, lozenge, triangle, and zigzag, as well as motifs drawn from nature like the palm tree, fish scale, and bird to embellish their textiles and jewelry. Islamic styles also gradually sifted through and were incorporated into their designs. Although they vary from place to place, these traditional patterns form a common symbolic language in the arts across the rural and urban Berber communities of North Africa.

Weaving was a significant feature of economic and social life. Wool was the main material of woven textiles made in the western part of North Africa, while linen and (from Roman times) cotton were major products of Egypt. In rural areas these textiles catered for the needs and customs of small agricultural and nomadic communities that were essentially tribal. Production relied on locally available materials, such as wool or goat and camel hair, and on natural dyes until the introduction of aniline dyes from Europe from the middle of the nineteenth century. Products included tent and home furnishings, rugs, blankets, cushions, saddle-cloths, and items of clothing. The latter were made in simple shapes that avoided the need to cut into cloth. Weaving, like spinning, was mostly in the hands of women. Techniques varied from group to group. Berbers, for example, used a vertical single-heddle loom, while the Bedouin, although they were often their close neighbors, preferred the ground loom.

In rural areas, people continued to wear traditional clothing such as rectangular wrappers, headshawls, and straight-sided tunics. Urban markets, however, demanded more cosmopolitan dress styles, and materials that could be cut and sewn to produce fashionable, shaped garments. Taste in embroidery patterns varied between town and country. In the rural areas, women produced embroidery that was spontaneous and lively. Using silk, wool, or cotton thread, wedding dresses and ceremonial shawls were embellished with patterns drawn from the natural environment and that reflected deep-seated community beliefs. In the towns, on the other hand, designs tended to be formal and predetermined, following an established composition, and regular repeating patterns were common. Algiers and Fez became renowned for their distinctive Turkish-influenced work on ceremonial shawls and domestic furnishings.[2]

There are common themes running through the decorative vocabulary of textiles and jewelry across North Africa. Techniques, forms, and patterns display the homogeneity that comes from having a shared history, religion, and cultural experience. But all forms of ornamentation reflect the beliefs, experience, and working environment of the culture that creates them, and each tribe, region, town, or oasis produced variants and differences in terms of a local style of craftwork and decoration. The jewelry and dress of Siwa Oasis in the Western Desert is a notable example of such a unique tradition. Until recently, little attempt has been made to record the different traditions that exist across North Africa or to collect examples of costumes and ornamentation—except, fortunately, from Siwa.[3]

The Oasis

2 History and Tradition

Siwa Oasis is situated in the heart of Egypt's Western Desert, some three hundred kilometers south of the Mediterranean coast and about five hundred and fifty kilometers west of the Nile Valley. It also lies forty-five kilometers from the Libyan border, and the Libyan oasis of Jaghbub to the northwest is one of Siwa's closest neighbors. In ancient times Siwa was called Sekht-am, meaning 'palm land.' The Greek colonists—and Alexander the Great—referred to the oasis as Zeus Ammon. In the fourteenth century Ibn Khaldun mentioned the Berber Ti-Swa people; and in the fifteenth, the Arab historian al-Maqrizi called the oasis Santaryah, noting that it had springs, palm gardens, olives, figs, and other fruit, and that its people suffered much from the djinn. He described its people as Berbers, speaking a language called "siwiyah" that resembled the language of a major tribe, the Zanata.[4] By the seventeenth century the use of its present name, Siwa, had become accepted.

Berber peoples have been characterized as being independent, private, and resistant to central authority. Indeed, they called themselves Imazighen, 'noble and free men.' They were and are still nomads, seasonal nomads, or settled farmers. The Berbers are the indigenous inhabitants of North Africa, and they still comprise scattered communities within a vast area from Morocco to Siwa. They may now be a minority in the Maghreb and geographically isolated, but the huge

13

expanse of territory covered by Berber speakers affirms the size of the area that they earlier dominated.

The people of Siwa are the most easterly of the Berbers, and they still speak the Berber dialect that distinguishes them from the rest of the population of the Egyptian Western Desert, whose mother tongue is Arabic. Berber, or Tamazight, belongs to the Afro-Asiatic language group, which embraces ancient Egyptian and Semitic languages, and it is their use of this language which above all defines the Siwans as Berbers. In recent years, the new road from the coast has brought in more visitors to the oasis, and the inhabitants have been fascinated to meet Berber speakers from distant areas of the Maghreb, and from as far afield as Paris. While Siwi, the variant spoken by the Siwans, and the Berber dialects of these visitors are often mutually incomprehensible, they are all recognized as being unmistakably Berber.

In classical times, Siwa was well known to the Greeks, who had expanded into Egypt and established trading settlements in the Nile Delta and eastern Libya, as a station on trade routes to the Nile Valley and across the Sahara, and as a source of dates *(teenee)*, palm wine, olives, and olive oil. They were also aware of the existence of the oracle of Amun-Ra in Siwa and equated the Egyptian god with Zeus. This led to what is the most significant recorded event in the history of the oasis when, in 332 BC, Alexander the Great traveled overland to visit the oracle. Later historians described how, in the temple court, priests carried a jeweled image of the god shoulder high in a gilded boat, so that Alexander could seek assurance that he was indeed the son of the deity. The oracle tactfully confirmed that he was.

After Alexander's death, the oracle continued to be influential under the Ptolemies, although it declined during the Roman domination of Egypt that followed the death of Cleopatra. It is likely that the oracle coexisted with Christianity until at least the sixth century when the Emperor Justinian ordered the closure of the remaining pagan temples. There are no records as to when Siwa converted to Islam, but this is believed to have been before the end of the seventh century.[5] It is said that the Arab geographer al-Idrisi in the twelfth century noted that the people of Santariyah were Muslims with an imam as their religious leader.

Siwa has its own venerated patron saint—Sidi Suleiman—whose tomb is beside the new mosque in the center of the town. Many miracles are associated with his name or attributed to his influence. For example, a story tells of the saint walking near the town when he grew thirsty. He

2. The ancient town of Aghurmi built around the Temple of the Oracle (1930s). *Royal Geographical Society.*

tapped the ground with his staff, and water immediately gushed from the spot. Another recounts that when an enemy army was approaching the town, instead of organizing a defense, Sidi Suleiman led the inhabitants into the mosque to pray. As a result of his prayers for divine intervention, the enemy host disappeared in the sands and was never seen again.

Life for the settled communities of the Western Desert in early times was remarkable for its insecurity and danger. An old Siwan manuscript kept by one of the families in the oasis describes how the oasis suffered so badly from Arab and Bedouin raids at the beginning of the thirteenth century that there were only forty men remaining. Indeed, attacks by the desert Bedouin in search of foodstuffs and loot in the form of the women's silver ornaments were a feature of desert life for centuries. It was in order to protect themselves that the inhabitants constructed defensive works at Shali, the heart of the present town of Siwa. Leadership was vested in the hands of a council of the sheikhs of all the tribes, *al-agwad*, which met at the Bab Inshal, the gate that provided the sole and secret entrance to the town. The council of sheikhs settled disputes, passed judgments, and decided punishments, which were the duty of the town crier (the *boab*) to administer. Anyone who failed to join a funeral procession, for example, would receive a certain number of strokes with a stick. Fines could be paid in baskets of dates. Some of the old laws and rules of conduct that are conducive to social order, such as banning loud music close to the town, are

3. A sheikh, probably of Aghurmi
(1920s). *Royal Geographical Society.*

still enforced. Another example is that a wedding will be postponed if a neighbor or member of the tribe dies.

From the time they moved into Shali, the fortunes of the Siwans changed for the better and their numbers increased. Until the eighteenth century, Siwa remained a remote appendage of the Ottoman province of Egypt, recognizing the authority of the caliph but remaining a semi-independent community. However, at the beginning of the nineteenth century, the brilliant and ruthless Ottoman viceroy of Egypt, Muhammad Ali, began to expand his authority over the formerly politically independent inhabitants of the Western Desert. His objective was to dominate the oases and thus control the trading routes. As a consequence, Siwa effectively lost its independence in 1820 when an Egyptian army attacked the fortress of Shali and raked it with cannon fire, killing thirty-three Siwan defenders. However, the spirit of independence reasserted itself and in succeeding years the inhabitants made intermittent attempts

4. The old town of Shali (1930s). *Royal Geographical Society.*

at resistance. There were short intervals of freedom before Egyptian troops returned to re-impose central authority, but the overall result was decades of lawlessness which undermined both the prosperity and stability of the area.

Today in Siwa, there are six Eastern tribes and three Western tribes, and the town itself is geographically divided into the East and the West. The Western tribes are Shihayam, Awlad Musa, and Sarahena. The Eastern tribes are Zanayn, al-Hadadin, Lehamudet, al-Jawasis, Sharameta, and Aghurmi. The only Arab Bedouin tribe, al-Shihaybat, lives in Maraqi, the area in the far west of the depression.

The division between the families of the East and the West was manifested in disputes that led to fights in which all fit men participated. These 'wars,' as the Siwans described them, were organized, disciplined incidents, and an altercation might persist for some days. To start hostilities, a sheikh sounded a drum and the groups assembled to fight the battle, supported by the women. A man *(ogeed)* could fire his gun only once—a reflection of the fact that it was a single-shot musket and of the restraining ritual underlying these events. In 1826, a sheikh told the French traveler Cailliaud that "these little wars taught them to brave the Bedouins, to despise death, and to preserve their independence."[6]

Between these short-lived bouts of armed aggression, the inhabitants managed to live fairly harmoniously together in the confined space of the old town. When the community was faced with invasions or danger from outside forces, such as marauding Bedouin, internal rivalries were forgotten and the Siwans formed a united front to repel the danger. When I was staying in Siwa in 1999 people said there was still a little rivalry between these two groups, although the town council had recently declared, "there is no East and there is no West." Before 1922 when the fights ceased, Easterners (al-Faia), and Westerners (al-Takhseeb) would not readily marry one another. Now they may do so. Likewise, although they still prefer not to mix, Westerners might live in the East, and Easterners in the West.

In the nineteenth century, the Senoussi Brotherhood, an Islamic sect based in Jaghbub in Libya, began to exercise its influence on Siwa and the surrounding region. The political and religious impact of the Brotherhood was noted by the German explorer Rohlfs, who visited Siwa in 1869 and in 1874. He found the Senoussi Brothers inspiring the spiritual lives of people, acting in the role of peacemakers in the feuds between the East and the West, and encouraging marriages between the warring factions.[7] A new Muslim order called al-Madiniya spread among the Easterners and is said to have complemented rather than hindered the Senoussiya movement, which gathered strength especially among the families of the Westerners.

Siwa may have remained remote, inaccessible, and culturally self-sufficient during this period, certainly from the point of view of individual inhabitants, but by the beginning of the twentieth century its political independence was being steadily eroded. The increasing involvement of the British in Egypt's government improved the Egyptian Frontier Administration and extended the influence of the central government. In addition, technical improvements in communications—notably the introduction of the telegraph, the automobile, and ultimately, the airplane—advanced the process even further.

The isolation of Siwa was further undermined, albeit temporarily, by the impact of two world wars. The Senoussi Brothers, who saw the First World War as a way of challenging Egyptian–British influence, threw their lot in with the Turks, and mounted a desert guerrilla campaign in Egypt. Siwa temporarily became a remote base for the forces of independence, but at the end of the war, the British reoccupied the oasis and the situation returned to normal. The desert campaign of the Second World War put the spotlight on Siwa again. The oasis was an ideal base for British guerrilla operations. The Italians bombed the oasis, forcing the inhabitants to find shelter in the rock tombs of Gebel al-Mawta, and briefly occupied it before the British victory at al-Alamein brought withdrawal and defeat.

Siwa is now fully integrated into the Egyptian state, but a number of unique cultural and administrative structures remain. The people are divided into the tribes, or *qabila*s, of the East and the West. Each Siwan tribe has a sheikh who is elected by its male members, even though this headship usually descends in one family from father to son and lasts for life. The sheikh mostly deals with the problems and disputes of his clan members in his own house, which is, accordingly, usually busy with visitors. Local anthropologist Fathi Malim says that the meeting with the sheikh, which is called a *me'ad*, can take many days and is always conducted with generosity and politeness until justice and peace are attained. "Essentially," he writes, "the sheikh should be wealthy—so that he can afford hospitality—married and wise, fair and just, and be respected by children and families even in old age."[8] For issues outside his control, the sheikh may advise an inhabitant to approach the police, or in another instance, the police may refer an inhabitant to the sheikh. Sheikhs have perhaps less power than before, but they form part of an advisory council that supports the mayor, who is the local representative of central government appointed by the governor in Marsa Matrouh.

3 The Oasis of Siwa

Siwa lies in a depression close to the Egyptian–Libyan border. The depression, which is in the shape of a pennant, stretches for eighty kilometers from east to west, and ranges from nine kilometers, north to south in the west, to twenty-five kilometers, in the east. Palm gardens, olive trees, salt lakes, limestone cliffs, and fresh water pools typify the landscape. Most of the population lives in the vicinity of Siwa town, close to springs and date and olive groves; the rest inhabit villages scattered throughout the depression.

One hundred and thirty kilometers northeast of Siwa town, in a remote valley surrounded by steep cliffs and rocks, is the small oasis of al-Gara (or Qaret Umm al-Sughayyar, which means 'Mother of the Little One'). The people of al-Gara are of African slave descent. They lived in a village perched on a rock reached by a steep and twisting path until the 1970s, when they moved to lower ground. The government later re-housed the families in cement-block homes and when I stayed in Siwa in 1999, the houses were being supplied with free electricity from sunset until 11:00 p.m. and a water supply was obtained from taps outside each house. Although, like Siwa, al-Gara was on a main caravan route linking the desert interior to the coast, and the east, it has always been a poor relation because of its isolated situation and the small size of its community, which eked out an existence through trading dates and baskets with travelers.

5. View over the oasis. *Vyacheslav Argenburg (via VascoPlanet.com).*

Today al-Gara numbers about 320 people. Its date and olive farmers benefit from government subsidies, and both men and women participate in making baskets for their own use and for the tourist industry, which can be found in craft shops in Siwa.

In addition to the settled peoples of the oases, the population of the Western Desert includes Bedouin tribes who herded camels, goats, and sheep along the Mediterranean coast and into the hinterland. The Awlad Ali Bedouin, who migrated into Egypt from Libya, possibly at the end of the seventeenth century, maintained links with Siwa and developed dependent economies, exchanging their livestock for Siwan dates, and using items of each other's crafts. Nowadays however, following a process of settlement in the nineteenth and twentieth centuries, the Bedouin have changed to a sedentary way of life. There are some Bedouin living today in Siwa town and west of Siwa in Bahiydeen and Maraqi, and there are large populations on the north coast in Marsa Matrouh, Sidi Barani, and Sollum.

The same period has also seen a dramatic increase in Siwa's size and a rise in the population to an estimated 23,000. This expansion carries the threat that the original Berber population will be overwhelmed and the Berber identity diluted. Nevertheless, Siwans still make up the majority of the population, and their artistic products—baskets, pottery, and

6. The village of al-Gara (1930s). *Royal Geographical Society.*

embroidery—remain distinctively Siwan, and Berber, although their character is changing fast in response to the tourist market.

The depression in which Siwa is located is eighteen meters below sea level. Underground water contained within sandstone beds lies close to the surface, and the water-bearing strata give rise to numerous springs and cultivated date gardens *(ateelun)*, around which people have traditionally made their homes. There is no shortage of water in Siwa and at least two hundred springs have been in use for centuries. However, the fact that Siwa lies below sea level leads to problems of drainage. Rainstorms, although rare, have always led to flash floods and problems of wastage which have been made worse by the fact that few of the new wells drilled by farmers since the mid-twentieth century were equipped to control the flow. Farmers may only need to irrigate for one or two days every fortnight, which means that for the rest of the time thousands of gallons of unused well water leak steadily into the salt lakes or are lost through evaporation.

In these lakes, the percentage of salt is high so that when the level of the water rises the surrounding area is encrusted with a white residue. Not only does this salinity restrict the possibilities of agriculture, but it permeates the dry mud bricks with which traditional homes are constructed, making them damp and in need of constant repair. Likewise, it

7. The salt lakes. *Vyacheslav Argenburg (via VascoPlanet.com)*.

has prevented the development of marine life in Siwa's lakes. There are no boats, and no traditional fishing industry, in spite of attempts to stock the lakes with fish. To tackle the problem of drainage and salinity, a land reclamation project was established in 1960 encompassing all five desert oases. The project was part of a program to open new land in the Western Desert, to improve the life of the people, and to draw the Siwans and the Bedouin into the Egyptian state. The living conditions of the peoples of the Western Desert improved, but Siwa's problems of salinity and drainage proved difficult to solve.

In recent years the government has been finding solutions. The newer wells drilled since the 1940s are being capped, cement canals are being constructed to carry water to irrigate the gardens, and sand is being built up around the lakes so that water is contained. When I was in Siwa in 2005, some of the new wells were being closed and replaced by one large, deep well shared by as many as fifteen families, who would be able to open the well to irrigate their land whenever they required water.

With no less than 200,000 date palms growing in the oasis it is not surprising that for centuries the economy has been dominated by dates. In addition to providing a surplus product, their high yield has always ensured that the inhabitants have a nutritious staple diet. There used to be three date markets in Siwa and, in the 1920s, C.D. Belgrave, who was district officer for Siwa, described them as

Large walled in squares where every merchant and family have a space to spread their dates for sale; one of them is common, the other two belong to east and west respectively. There is a little house by the entrance of each market where an old Sudanese watchman lives, paid in kind by contributions from everybody who uses the market.[9]

In November, December, and January thousands of camels and their riders from other parts of Egypt and the west used to descend on Siwa's date markets to buy fresh or dried dates or to barter them for their own merchandise. There was a tradition that while the men were in the date market, they could help themselves to as many dates as they could eat on the spot for free, but they were not allowed to take any away without paying.

These days, unfortunately, the date markets can no longer be seen. The farmers take their dates to be processed and packed in local factories, resulting in less wastage and higher profits. At the beginning of the harvest, a farmer told me, he might get 125 piasters[10] for a kilo of dates. At the end, when the factories have taken all the dates they require, they sell at 70 piasters per kilo. Siwan dates, especially the Saidi, the 'king of dates,' are considered to be the best in Egypt and are also exported to Libya.

For centuries the date gardens, the *ateelun*, were worked by male laborers known as *zaggala*, who spent their time trimming, fertilizing, harvesting, and pollinating the date palms. They were 'propertyless' bachelors of between twenty and forty years of age, many being Sudanese or Nigerian slaves who came with slave caravans going to Egypt, and remained in the oasis. They slept in huts outside the town walls. The word *zaggal* probably meant 'warrior,' for as well as being agricultural laborers they were used as guards against the danger of Bedouin raids. They were paid in kind with quantities of dates and barley at the end of the year, and provided with cotton clothes for summer and with a thick wool tunic, a *jubit*, for winter.

The laborers toiled from sunrise to sunset, but they were well known for their jollity, and sang as they worked. At night they sang and danced under the stars to the drum, flute, and castanets, and became merry drinking *lagbi* made from the sap of the palm tree. Some of their liveliest songs and dances are said to have originated from the slaves who brought music and drumming to their new setting. The term *zaggal* has now lost its original meaning, and the name merely means 'farm worker.' Indeed,

8. View across al-Khosh date market (1930s). *Royal Geographical Society.*

any young man who has a strong physique, even if he is rich, may be referred to as *zaggal*, but Siwan music groups are still called *zaggala*.

The date and olive gardens stretch from Siwa's outer limits almost to the central square. The date palms stand in beds, or *houd*s, that are connected to supply ditches during irrigation. There are a number of private springs and water pumps for the exclusive use of their owners, but many gardens are watered from a communal central spring. According to Siwan archaeologist Dr. Abd El-Aziz Aldumairy:

In the last 500 years, water has been traditionally allotted to landowners under the supervision of a 'hassab' or 'regulator', who was paid either in dates or water. Any disputes over water were handled by the 'wakil', or trustee, who kept the written agreements, which he memorized as well.[11]

The water allotment for each garden used to be timed by a local system called *wagaba*.

9. Traditional Siwan houses (1930s). *Royal Geographical Society.*

The palm trees are locally known as *shagara tayiba* ('the good trees') because so much is extracted from them. They have always provided the inhabitants (and their animals) with dates of various qualities, with the drink called *lagbi*, and with *gumar*—the white heart of the palm, usually taken from a weak male tree they will probably lose—which is a delicacy enjoyed at weddings and other feasts. Palm logs are the basic construction material of the traditional mud house. They are used to make windows, doors, and door locks, and beams that support the upper floor and roof of mud houses; and for the *dulula*, the pleasant sun shelter with a flat roof on pillars of mud that is constructed in the garden. Palm leaves are used by the men and the women to make their baskets, and children make playthings, such as stilts and swings, from the branches.

There are 40,000 olive trees in Siwa and in former times olive oil was produced in family-owned presses. It was burned in lamps, and used in the grooming of the skin and hair as well as being a foodstuff. Most of the presses have now been replaced by olive oil factories, but when I was staying in Siwa in 1999, two survived and were still patronized by many of the inhabitants who valued the high quality of the oil. There are many sayings and jokes about the benefits of olive oil for both man and beast.

Men traditionally spent much of their time cultivating the dates and olives on which the prosperity of the oasis depended. Their other activities included carpentry, building houses, stone masonry, blacksmithing, and silverwork for women's jewelry. Today Siwan men do a variety of jobs.

They work in the date and olive gardens, local factories, government offices, shops, carpentry, blacksmithing, the building trades, and tourism and hotels. They are also responsible for making the heavy-duty 'plaited' baskets that are needed to carry the produce of the gardens, and the palm sling *(idhar)* that supports an individual as he climbs a tree to prune branches or cut down dates.

About seventy percent of Siwans today own at least one palm garden, often located some distance from where they live. The male members of the family are responsible for the cultivation of the date palms, and at harvest time as many as a thousand migrant laborers from Upper Egypt have been called on to help throughout the oasis. The local laborers who work in the gardens today are relatively well paid—as much, it is said, as schoolteachers. New products like squash, figs, and apples are also being grown in the oasis, mostly by male migrants from the Nile Valley. Today there are said to be about ten wealthy Siwan families who, as well as owning large numbers of date and olive gardens, are involved in such enterprises as hotels, shops, supermarkets, and new land development projects. At the beginning of the twentieth century there were two rich families, one in the east and one in the west, who would have had about one hundred feddans[12] and employed three hundred laborers. Nowadays, the average garden is around fifty feddans.

10. A typical donkey cart. *Royal Geographical Society.*

To cover distances within the oases, a reliable form of transport is needed; in Siwa it is the donkey cart. These are to be seen everywhere, moving people within the town and taking them to the date gardens.

Siwan women do not work in the gardens. They are active in the home doing domestic chores and embroidery, or making baskets for their own use or to sell to tourists. It may be that historically the surplus wealth gained through trading dates freed the women from agricultural work, and allowed them to develop their domestic craft skills and conform to the Islamic tradition of keeping women out of the public sphere. Women do, however, enjoy outings to the gardens with their children. There, on pleasant, cool, sunny days after the harvest, young boys scale the palm trees to shake the remaining dates from the trees while the women and girls select and gather dates from the ground for their donkeys. Most families own at least one donkey, or *izeat*, and a lot of human effort is required in maintaining it.

Women's Crafts

Most of Siwa's crafts were and are produced by women. Embroidery *(tatris)* is an exceptional skill and form of expression. The fine stitching that adorns women's ceremonial clothes celebrates personal and collective identity, and also reveals status. The regular, well-ordered lines of motifs relate to horizontal lines of patterns found on North African textiles and carry enduring historical links.

Fine baskets and clay pots were made for domestic use and for exchange before mass-produced crockery and plastic goods became readily available. Achieving a high standard was a source of satisfaction and pride, and exceptional craftswomen gained considerable prestige in the community.

Baskets

The women's baskets and trays, made of fine coils, were as essential in the home as the rustic plaited baskets made by the men were in the gardens and marketplace. Women make their baskets using a tool called an *astin* and a sheaf of palm fiber they stitch down with thin strips of palm leaf. The men make their heavy-duty palm-leaf baskets and floor mats *(labrash)* by plaiting five long strips, which they then coil and stitch to the required shape.[13]

Women traditionally made about ten different kinds of coiled basket designed for different purposes. Some of these baskets had lids, others

11 and 12. (Left) A bride's basket *margunah*; (right) a palm leaf tray, *tiset*, used for chickpeas, peanuts, and sweets. *Musée d'ethnographie, Geneva.*

were open. Some baskets were richly adorned with worsted and silk thread, green and red dyes, mother-of-pearl *(sadaf)* buttons, and red leather. Motifs called 'water snake,' 'chicken's foot' (also a common motif in Libyan weaving), and a checkered pattern called *iharuzang* were used for embellishment. The decorative tubes of red leather below the rim were probably once threaded with rope handles. There were basketmakers so skilled they could make baskets that would hold water, and there was still a handful of these exceptional craftswomen working in the oasis when I first went to stay there.

One decorated conical-lidded basket, called a *margunah ntghara*, is still made to contain bread. It is a very large bread-basket, made to be used at weddings. Indeed, a lavishly decorated *margunah* is reserved for the bride. A flat tray, called a *tiset*, with a circle of red leather in the center and colored lines radiating from it like the rays of the sun, is for peanuts, chickpeas, or sweets. Large, plain baskets called *agnin* are used in the storeroom to hold such commodities as rice and grain. The *tadelt* is made for dates and olives.

Women also make plain, open baskets that act as measures for produce such as lentils, dates, rice, and flour. Some of these are still used in the home. The standard measure is the *akodah* (or *saa*), which holds about two and a half kilos of soft juicy dates, or two kilos of dry dates. Another measure, the *arabu*, is a quarter the size of the *akodah*, and two other measures are half the size and a quarter the size of the *arabu*.

13. An official filling a basket measure with date stones to ensure the volume is correct.

Once the basket measure has been made it is taken to the Siwan official to certify that it is the correct size. This is done by pouring a specified quantity of date stones into the basket, and people say of the official, 'he knows every stone.' If they spill over, the basket is too small, and has to be given to one of the women of the official's family who will add to the rim until not even one stone is spilled. When it is the correct size, a metal tag with a seal (*atba* in Siwi and *khatem* in Arabic), inscribed with the year, is fixed over the rim. If the basket, say a flour measure, later stretches as a result of frequent breadmaking, the woman will send it to be checked. If it is found to be too big, a couple of rows will be removed from the rim and it will be stamped with the new date. This practice still goes on, but when I visited the workshop, I was told that whereas in the past they were very busy, fewer and fewer baskets were now being sent to be stamped—only one every three days (at a cost of five Egyptian pounds).

14. A man's woolen tunic *(jubit)* being woven on a single-heddle loom (1920s). *Royal Geographical Society.*

Weaving

The only garment spun and woven in Siwa used to be the thick woolen tunic called a *jubit* (in Arabic *jubba*) worn by male laborers. It was made on the vertical, single-heddle Berber loom. Ahmed Heda, in his mid-seventies, told me that his father, a local landowner, had attempted to set up a workshop to weave the women's more sophisticated indigo blue and white checked shawls, that are traditionally brought from Kerdassa, near the Pyramids in Cairo, but it had been too difficult.

The laborer's cream-colored *jubit* was decorated with a colorful pattern of short horizontal lines. It was woven as a long rectangle with a hole in the middle for the head. The sides were then stitched up leaving wide openings for the arms. There was an old superstition that the wearer would outlive a garment if he put it on and held a palm leaf in his mouth while it was stitched up.

Some Siwans still find the robust traditional tunic the most convenient garment for work in the gardens even in the summer, and two hand-woven striped woolen cloths are still used in breadbaskets. Both items are also sold to tourists, the cloths now also embellished with new materials and patterns to please foreign visitors.

Pottery

Just as there used to be many different types of domestic basket made by women, so there were women potters making a variety of unglazed pots for use in the home. They were used for storing water or oil, for cooking, washing hands, drinking vessels, burning incense, holding the fire to heat a room, and for ritual purposes. Before people had electric light in the home there were little oil lamps in the shape of a foot to provide illumination.

Two different clays were used: a dry desert clay, to which sand was added, and garden clay. Walter Cline (who lived in Siwa for a few months in the winter of 1926–27) also refers to the former as 'edible clay' because it was eaten by pregnant women "to give their offspring a dark complexion."[14] A large pot was roughly molded into shape, then turned and worked over the left hand. The walls were next built up to an even thickness on a cloth-covered tray on the knee. The vessel was left outside for a week to dry out, and then smoothed over with a stone. If decoration was needed, vertical linear patterns were painted in red slip around the outside before the pot was fired upside down over a fire made of olive wood.[15] When I stayed in Siwa, there were a small number of experienced, elderly women potters still making the traditional pots, most of which are now sold to tourists. They used red slip obtained from a seam in the rock of Takrur Mountain to paint designs around the sides.[16] The patterns, though they have

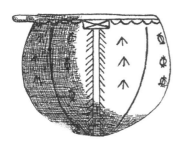

15. Decorated Siwan pots.

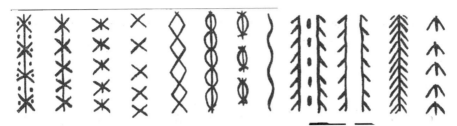

16. Embroidery stitches used on ceremonial clothes and depicted on pots. *Oric Bates.*

become simpler, are reminiscent of the lines of decorative stitches the Siwan women work over the surfaces of their ceremonial shawls and dresses and along the seams of trouser legs. It has been suggested that the vertical linear patterns painted on the pots represent seams on water-skins, thus evoking a previous nomadic lifestyle.[17]

The arrival of machine-made goods originally caused a decline in the local production of women's crafts, but the tourist industry produced a stimulus and as it increased the women began to produce handicrafts specifically to sell to the visitors. Work on handicrafts, whether for themselves or for tourists, begins when the women have finished the housework, at *itha* (about eleven o'clock in the morning). Any money they earn is entirely their own to spend as they wish. If the family is needy it goes toward the household income.

17. Siwan pots for sale in a tourist shop.

4 Camels and Cargoes

From earliest times, Siwa was a way station on the network of trade routes that crossed North Africa from north to south and from east to west. These routes were traversed by caravans of camels transporting a huge variety of commodities. They also brought travelers: merchants bound for distant markets, students heading for the *madrasa*s and al-Azhar, the university-mosque of Cairo, and pilgrims going on the Hajj. If they lacked ready money, they could carry trade goods, stowed on a carrier on the back of a camel, which would be bartered for dates and other necessities along the way. The farther they traveled, the higher the prices they could obtain for goods that seemed exotic but which had been bought cheaply at home.

From the Maghreb, the caravans carried sun-dried meat, silver jewelry, leather slippers, cloth and garments in wool and silk, and the produce of European metallurgy in the form of sword blades and needles. From Arabia and Egypt came grain, legumes, spices and incense, glass beads, mirrors, linen, cotton, clothes, and silks from further east. The largest caravans were those that crossed the Sahara from the south to Awjila in northeastern Libya, bringing slaves, ostrich feathers, and red leather from red goats of Sokoto in modern-day Nigeria. From there, they headed for Egypt, taking the eastward route through Siwa. Darfur in Sudan was an important source of both male and female slaves and remained so until the last quarter of the nineteenth century. Some former slaves stayed on in Siwa, as bonded laborers in the date gardens or as domestic servants in the old mud town.

Camel caravans had to cope with the natural hazards of desert travel such as shortages of water, sand storms, and burning days and freezing nights, but they also had to contend with raids from marauding Bedouin on the way. Arab and Berber nomads acted as caravan guides. True men of the desert, they preferred the inland desert routes via established oases to the coastal ones, even though it involved wearisome diversions to watering places. The bigger caravans were protected from raiders by armed guards, and would have had a leader who saw to the necessary discipline of the community and negotiated with the powers that be in the caravan stations. Traveling Muslim clerics were on hand to deal with the religious needs of the travelers, and preachers not only led daily prayers but wrote amulets and drew magic squares for good fortune.

Siwa's main route to the outside world was that which ran to the city of Marsa Matrouh on the Mediterranean, a distance of some three hundred kilometers. It was this route that formed the main line along which a tarmac road was built in the 1980s to provide Siwa with a motor link to the coast. In the days of camel caravans, it took walking camels ten days and trotting camels six days to complete this journey, with the travelers usually living on dates, camel milk, and water.

In 1906, the khedive of Egypt, Abbas Hilmi, traveled along this route to Siwa, with a vanguard of sixty-two camels and twenty Arab soldiers

18. Saharan caravan on the march. *Royal Geographical Society.*

followed by a main body comprising twenty-two horses, a mounted bodyguard, and 288 camels, live sheep, and fowls. In 1928 King Fuad made his visit by car escorted by the Camel Corps. To greet the king, Siwan men lined the streets, and the women gathered on the rooftops of houses clad in their festive clothes and silver jewelry. That night there was a firework display and film presentation, and Siwan men performed *zaggala* songs, music, and dances. Ahmed Fakhry says the people still talk about "the beautiful uniforms of the King's courtiers and his bodyguard" and the presents, which included swords, ceremonial robes, gold watches, and cashmere shawls for the sheikhs, and clothes and money for the poor.[18] After King Fuad's visit, improvements were made to the education system and to the production and processing of dates and a factory was built, advancing the Egyptianization of the oasis. In 1945 King Farouk made an informal visit to Siwa with friends in a convoy of desert cars. Rather disappointingly he was wearing shorts, an affront to the conservative morals of Siwans.

There were two routes linking Siwa and central Egypt to the east. The first was the Masrab Bahariya, a desolate desert track of three hundred kilometers going eastward and passing first through a string of oases then branching either east to the Nile Valley or northeast to Fayoum and Cairo. The second route was the Darb al-Dar. This headed northeast, crossed the escarpment at Naqd al-Megberi—a notorious place for ambushes during the age of camel transport—then swung in a wide loop to the oasis of al-Gara. It then headed southeast and east to the spring of al-Maghra on the edge of the Qattara Depression, then on to Wadi Natrun, famous as the site of ancient Coptic monasteries, then southeast to Kerdassa, and thence to Cairo. This is the route that Alexander followed when he returned from visiting Siwa. Muhammad Ali also used it as his invasion route when his troops subdued the oasis in 1820.

Camel caravans heading northwest from Siwa to Libya could take one of half a dozen tracks to the coast. Of these, most popular was one or other of the two tracks together referred to as the Thieves' Road. The main track was called the Road of the Brothers, or Masrab al-Ikhwan, named after the Senoussi Brotherhood, the religious sect that dominated the area in the nineteenth century. The Senoussi Brothers earned the gratitude of the merchants by establishing themselves as the protectors of the region and effectively guaranteeing the safe transport of goods. The second track, the Masrab al-Rukhba, leaves the main route ten kilometers from Siwa, and provides a deviation through the escarpment to the northwest via the

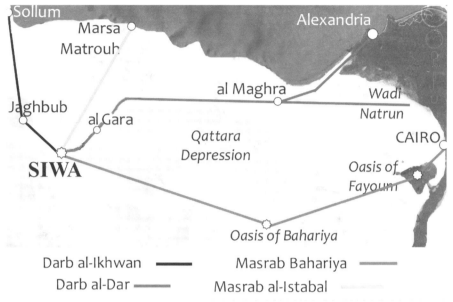

Darb al-Ikhwan ━━━ Masrab Bahariya ━━━
Darb al-Dar ━━ Masrab al-Istabal ┄┄┄

19. Camel routes around Siwa. *NASA.*

Naqb Mazouha (Pass of the Measure), before joining Road of the Brothers for its approach to Jaghbub.[19]

The transportation of produce and merchandise between Siwa and the Nile Valley and Libya was the responsibility of the Awlad Ali Bedouin. Latterly however, Siwans themselves also made trading journeys to the coast and Alexandria, to the oasis of Fayoum, and to Cairo, as well as to Fezzan and Jaghbub in Libya.

The journals of nineteenth- and early twentieth-century travelers provide a picture of the variety of merchandise being carried along these routes, the workings of the various trading centers, and the size and composition of the camel caravans. From the thirteenth to nineteenth centuries, the ancient trade routes to the Red Sea and back were frequented by North African pilgrims heading for, or returning from, Mecca. Frederick Horneman, writing in 1798, described how he traveled in such a caravan. He joined at Kerdassa on 5 September and, after a few days at al-Gara, arrived in Siwa on 21 September. At al-Gara, Horneman describes a few poor pilgrims from his caravan bartering their merchandise for dates: "Coming to a kind of market place, in its center, I observed bargain making with such eagerness, noise and altercation, that one should suppose the dealings to be of the first moment." The pilgrims' articles of trade were, however, "merely henna, hoechel [probably kohl], rings of lead or glass, and such like ornaments for women" and "a little shot and gunpowder."[20] To Horneman, who did not understand their significance, these goods seemed of little value, but the ornaments were needed by the women as important constituents of their jewelry ensemble. They would use kohl to outline their eyes, and the henna to decorate their skin and for medicinal remedies.

Cailliaud, writing at the beginning of the nineteenth century, was struck by the importance to Siwa of these caravans and noted that something like seven hundred camels arrived there annually from Egypt, one-third of which were carrying imports to be exchanged for dates; while another 350 camels came from Libya and the Maghreb for the same purpose. From Egypt came barley, dried legumes, and tobacco leaves, as well as Venetian glass beads, textiles, and small mirrors. From the Maghreb came sun-dried meat, sheep, and merchandise that included silver jewelry, tarbooshes, yellow Moroccan slippers, and woolen wraps.[21] There were silk robes for the rich Siwan landowners and their wives and families, and amulets for women and children and for men to pin inside their red Tunisian-made caps for protection against the evil eye and the djinn.

One hundred years later, Gertrude Simpson painted a similar picture: Items traded for dates included wheat, leather goods from Sudan, "many useful articles of dress; fancy fly whisks from Kufra; silver ornaments and bracelets of rare workmanship from the far West, and rugs, and sometimes shawls of Bedouin manufacture, besides arms, spices, coffee, mirrors, glass beads and other little hardware goods which they sell at great profit."[22] Steindorf, writing a few years before, included scissors, pigments, knives, soap, tea, and sugar.[23] Siwan women relied on certain prescribed pieces of jewelry imported from the west in addition to the local supply.

Many of the items of jewelry imported into Siwa were obtained as a result of direct barter in exchange for local produce. Some could, however, be bought in the shaded little shops located in the central square and dotted about the town. Belgrave, writing in the early 1920s, says that the shops were "hardly noticeable," there was "no display of goods, nothing in fact to distinguish a shop,"[24] though each was a general store selling more or less what the others sold. As a result, each family used the shop nearest to home. From a room on the ground floor, the merchant sold produce such as beans, flour, rice, tea, sugar out of sacks and cases, and tins of oil. *Saa* baskets holding specified quantities of these items were used as measures. In a corner there were "some rolls of calico and a bundle of colored handkerchiefs hung on a nail from the ceiling." Visiting the shops, he was aware of "a queer, rather pleasant smell, a potpourri of incense, spices, herbs, olive oil and coffee"[25] which pervaded them. Women customers purchased their attire on the upper floor of the shop, which was reached through the side entrance. Here the merchant's wife or mother sold

> 'kohl' for darkening the eyes, henna for ornamenting fingers and hands, silver ornaments, soft scarlet leather shoes and boots, blue cotton material manufactured at Kerdassa, near Gizeh, grey shawls, silks for embroidery, dyes for coloring baskets and very expensive flashy silk handkerchiefs made in Manchester, which they (wore) around their heads when indoors. Some of the merchants' wives (sold) charms and amulets besides clothes.[26]

The importation of coins, via the merchants and pilgrims coming by camel caravan, was the source for the supply of silver that provided the raw material for the production of the women's jewelry. After a good harvest, silver coins assigned for jewelry, rather than buried in the ground as family funds for security, would be sent to the local silversmiths to be melted down.

In 1920, Belgrave saw the Siwans using Egyptian coins in the shops, "the silver being much preferred to the paper currency."[27] These were the silver piasters, or *qirsh*, that were similar in appearance to Ottoman coins and were the basic unit of currency in the country. They had the *tughra*, or emblem, of the sultan on one side, and *Misr*, Arabic for Egypt, on the other. Coins produced after 1922 showed the head of King Fuad I. European coins had also been traded alongside local Egyptian and Ottoman coins for centuries before. Spanish, Dutch, French, and English coins, whose silver or gold content could be guaranteed, had been used as trading currencies from the sixteenth century onward.

Austrian silver thalers and Spanish and Mexican silver dollars were widely used in North Africa and were heavily in demand for melting down to make jewelry. The most valued and distinctive of the foreign coins traded across North Africa was, however, the Austrian Maria Theresa thaler. Issued first in 1741, it showed a portrait of the young empress on one side and the Hapsburg arms on the other. The coin was restruck after the death of Maria Theresa in 1780, and that date was set on the coin for the next two hundred years. Its popularity rested on its intrinsic value, the reliability of its silver content, and the familiar comely image of the empress, displaying the mature bloom of womanhood. A jeweled tiara adorned her curly hair, and a brooch gathered the neckline of her silk dress revealing her ample bosom. The edge was inscribed *Justitia et Clementia* (Justice and Clemency) to discourage the dishonest practice of taking silver clippings. The Maria Theresa thaler, and the Mexican 'pillar' dollar that showed the Pillars of Hercules, were also valued as amuletic ornaments, and were integrated into necklaces, belts, or headdresses—though not in Siwa.

20. A silver 'Pillar' dollar.

21. A Maria Theresa silver dollar.

5 Siwa Town

After a long bus journey through the flat, stony desert from Marsa Matrouh on the coast, the road climbs and enters a surrealist landscape such as Yves Tanguy or Salvador Dali might have dreamt up. An earlier visitor, H.V. Morton, compared it to "the mountains of the moon," with "weird dead hills, each one carved into some improbable shape, a cone, a cube, a queer isolated pinnacle, a ridge that from a distance looked like a battlemented castle with turrets."[28] The bus then descends through a ravine, and turns suddenly to reveal the immense carpet of Siwa Oasis. After hours of gazing out at the yellow desert, the green palms and silver-edged lakes are a refreshing and welcoming sight.

In no time, the bus draws up in the central square of the town. Towering above, the ruins of the old fortified settlement of Shali are silhouetted, against the early evening sky. The square is busy with donkey carts (*carusas*), full of clover (*berseem*), or other kinds of produce, and small wooden carriages (*caretas*) with families returning from visits to relations or friends. The latter are driven by men or young boys and are filled with women swathed in blue-grey shawls and teenage girls with large pastel colored headscarves streaming behind.

Along one side of the square, brightly lit fruit and vegetable stalls can be seen, piled high with oranges, lemons, limes, tomatoes, potatoes,

22. Shali square.

zucchini, and onions. There are small open-air restaurants, patronized in the cooler seasons of the year by young foreign backpackers, Egyptian visitors who arrive by coach, and German tourists with their camper vans parked outside. From many restaurants, tourist shops, and hotels, guides will arrange trips into the desert—to Bir Wahed to hunt for fossils, to watch the sunset from Fathnis Island on the salt lake of Birket Siwa, or to see *zaggala* perform their songs and dances. Tourists can travel around the oasis by *careta* or bicycle—bicycle shops in Siwa do good business renting and repairing. Visitors can wander down palm-fringed lanes that are mostly free of motor traffic, through the palm groves to the ancient sites of the Temple of the Oracle, the Temple of Umm Ubayda, the nearby Spring of the Sun (Ayn al-Gubah), and the tombs of the Mountain of the Dead (Gebel al-Mawta).

The area in and around Siwa's town square is filled with small shops with goods spilling out onto the street. There are general stores selling bedding and clothes, stationery, plastic buckets, and piles of identically printed crockery and enamelware from China that have largely replaced the handmade pottery traditionally used by Siwan households. There are grocery stores, a butcher's bench with long pieces of meat hanging from

23. A row of shops and workshops with donkey carts.

hooks, shops selling attractively arranged boxes of Siwan dates and bottles of green olives, and a colorful shop selling herbs and homeopathic medicines.

For the tourist, there are shops selling: silver jewelry from glass cases; rings, coins, and old jewelry components from metal bowls; round silk-decorated baskets with conical lids; brightly decorated baskets from al-Gara; clay bowls, oil lamps, and incense burners painted with red linear patterns; red and cream striped rugs woven by Awlad Ali Bedouin women; and embroidered textiles and garments made by Siwans. The owners struggle to keep the embroidered wedding dresses free of dust by dampening the sand that wafts through the open shop frontage. In

24. A fruit and vegetable stall.

25. A butcher's bench. *Royal Geographical Society.*

preparation for the religious or local festivals, or *eid*s, during which hundreds of Egyptians descend on Siwa, shopkeepers will pile high their banks of Bedouin rugs, and Siwan women will seek out their old silver jewelry, beads, and traditional clothes so that their children can take them to the tourist shops to sell.

The walls of some of these shops, like those of some restaurants and the local photographer's studio, are decorated with brightly painted murals depicting the foliage and fruit of the date palm and the olive tree, desert landscapes, or the ancient Siwan sites under a blazing sun. Many of these pictures are the work of the young artist Yousef Ibrahim Eissa, the first Siwan to have exhibited his pictures in his hometown and in galleries in Egyptian cities. Coming from a family of blacksmiths, Yousef's decision to become an artist was unusual in Siwa. When he began to paint around the town, he remembers being told to "get a proper job" and "go and work in the gardens." And when his family finally accepted his career choice, his father had to buy paints for him as far afield as Alexandria. "Bringing artists' materials to Siwa at that time," he told me, "was like bringing stones from the moon." One of his first commissions came from a newly married couple for a wall painting for the bridal room, the *taarfet narus*. Many of his subsequent commissions were related to marriage. And when a friend was

26. A tourist shop.

getting married, instead of helping to repair or decorate his house which is the custom in Siwa, he would paint a wall picture as a wedding gift, the theme "taken from nature—a spring, flowers, trees—for a beautiful future." Other requests include decorating a *carusa* and painting a mural on a wall of a water factory. Nowadays, people are familiar with his pictures and there is great interest in them.

The center of Siwa is dominated by the old, ruined, fortified mud town of Shali (meaning 'the town'), which rises straight from the ground, crowning a rock. According to local history and tradition as recorded in the Siwan manuscript mentioned in chapter 2, Shali was founded in AH 600 (AD 1203) when the seven

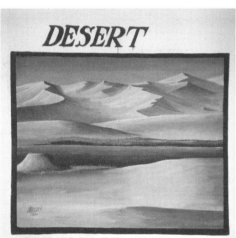

27. Yousef's wall picture.

28. Down the steps from Shali to the tourist shops.

families of the original settlement at Aghurmi decided to move to a new site where they built a fortified village to afford them protection from desert invaders. Over the years, its walls have been molded by occasional heavy rainfall into a stack of steep pinnacles and ragged towers. As the walls continue to collapse, there is serious concern that this monument to Siwa's past and a paramount tourist attraction will crumble away completely, unless significant conservation work is undertaken.

In the past, the town was enclosed by defensive walls that formed great battlements soaring into the sky. As the population increased, the inhabitants were forced to build upward until the houses had reached several stories high. Describing Shali in the 1920s, Belgrave wrote "The houses are built one above the other against the face of the rock . . . . on the top of the old ones . . . . house upon house, street upon street, and quarter upon quarter. . . . Fathers built houses for their sons above the parental abode, till their great-grandsons reached a dizzy height on the topmost battlements."[29] Doors cut from palm logs opened out of these

29. A Siwan house.

tenements into a network of steep, winding passages and tunnels, and from these pathways could be heard "the subdued hum of human voices, from invisible people, and the perpetual sound of stone grinding-mills, above, below and all around."[30] After the conquest of Siwa by the forces of Muhammad Ali in the 1820s, the fear of raids from desert invaders receded and permission was given by *al-agwad* council, composed of the sheikhs of the tribes, for the inhabitants of Shali to live outside the walls. The sheikhs and wealthy merchants were the first to leave the old town, building large houses at the foot of Shali or among the palm groves. Others followed, and the town steadily began to spread.

In 1926, particularly heavy rain caused the tall, old mud houses in Shali to collapse or become unsafe, and more people moved to build in the new settlements outside the walls. There was a similar exodus in 1969. When I was in Siwa in 2000, there was still a handful of families living and maintaining their houses in Shali. Building houses on the floor of the oasis meant that conservation was easier, but walls still needed to be constantly repaired and houses still occasionally collapsed when prolonged rainfall caused the salt crystals in the mud to dissolve and the walls to disintegrate.

30. A mosque on Shali.

The traditional Siwan house is made with thick mud walls and small doors and windows to keep the rooms cool in the heat of summer, and warm when the cold bites on sharp winter days and even colder nights. The traditional house has rounded corners and walls that slope gently inward to the flat roof made of split palm logs, palm thatch, and dried mud. Beams that support the upper floor and the roof often extend outside the walls of the house and are a distinctive feature of the architecture. The blocks of *kersheef*

31. A doorway with a representation of the sun and its rays.

of which the house is built are made of a mixture of mud and salt that is collected from the edges of the lakes, and the blocks are fixed using a kind of clay called *klact*. Liquid clay mixed with sand is plastered over the outside and inside walls of the house to give a smooth finish.

The exterior walls of many Siwan houses are painted a distinctive mineral blue by a bridegroom before the wedding, to bring him and his bride good luck and to protect them from the evil eye. The walls of some

32. An entrance hall.

houses are decorated with pictures of the Kaaba, the Great Mosque in Mecca, or pilgrim ships, to show that a resident has made the pilgrimage.

Generally speaking, Siwan houses are rectangular in shape and have two floors and an open roof space. Entrance to a traditional house is through a thick, low palm wood door fitted with a decorated wooden lock, which leads into a dark lobby. There will be a water jar *(zir)* by the door. A mud seat has been built in a discrete corner, and mud stairs go up to the next floor. Internal arrangements differ slightly, but usually on the ground floor there will be a visitors' room called a *maarbua* that is used only by men. At the back of the house will be storerooms for tools *(tiquat)* and for foodstuffs *(mahzen)* and a room for the donkey. The donkey's cart stands outside. The cooking area is behind the house and usually consists of a mud oven *(tabint)* and a small mud burner for pans *(emensi)*. Part of this space is roofed over with palm, to provide shade from the sun.

The mud stairway to the next floor leads into a wide, well-lit hall called a *stahnamas*. Hanging on the walls of the hall there is usually a prayer mat, a colorful, round palm-leaf tray, and a finely made basket decorated with silk tassels. A number of rooms will often lead off the hall. They have small windows that nevertheless bring in light and sun, and have wooden shutters but no glass. Some rooms have specific purposes, but will often double up as bedrooms with floor mattresses folded away in piles against a wall during the day. A talented young child might paint around the walls of the room shared with siblings, perhaps an attractive repeating pattern of flowers and leaves. Another room is reserved for a married son and his wife. The 'winter room' *(itgarfet enishti)* is a cozy place for the family to live in cold weather, with a basin of olive wood burning in the center. There is also a visitor's room that the women use. The last two rooms are frequently furnished with a large red, carved clothes chest *(senduq)* prominently placed in the room, and with cheerful red-striped rugs laid

33. Detail of an old Siwan house.

over palm matting, which will keep out the dust from the mud floor. There are often oblong, bright print cushions for sitting.

The upper floor is also the location of a shower room and a separate toilet, which in the past was just a hole in the floor that allowed the contents to collect in a room below where sand and ash were shovelled every day. Once a year the contents were removed to provide compost for the garden. Worn mud steps lead up to the open roof, which in summer is an ideal place to have dinner or sleep under the stars. A good impression of how these mud dwellings were built and functioned can be gained by visiting the Siwa House Museum in town.

Although with thick walls and high ceilings a traditional Siwan house is ideal for the climate, it is not easy to maintain. Most people would prefer to live in a modern house built from cement blocks, which are dry, permanent, and easier to clean. It is a cleaner environment in which to do embroidery and make baskets. Moving to such a house is also seen as a way of gaining status and keeping up with the 'Siwan Joneses' in the neighborhood. Indeed, a modern image is so important that at a public meeting a few years ago, a proposal to build houses using a strengthened mud material was rejected.

34. A modern building using mud, the traditional construction material.

Fearful of the consequences of this trend on Siwa's culture and tourist potential, the governate of Marsa Matrouh, as part of an Egyptian–Italian environmental program, has encouraged the construction of mud-brick buildings in the oasis. In the town there are now attractive public buildings that complement the traditional local architecture, such as the Banque du Caire, Siwa's first bank, established in 2005. There is a beautiful mud-brick hotel among the palm gardens some two hundred meters from Siwa's town square, and a local cooperative has recently created an atmospheric mud-brick hotel against the walls of Shali. About sixteen kilometers from Siwa, at the foot of Gebel Gafr overlooking the salt lake Birket Siwa, there is the first of these hotels, the Andrére Amellal, an environmentally sound 'hotel-village,' constructed from traditional materials and furnished with local crafts. Nearby is the al-Taziry ecolodge. This strategy seems to be working. Unsuitable colors for exterior decoration are no longer tolerated, and people are encouraged to finish their modern houses with a coat of liquid clay. When building a modern house, instead of demolishing the old mud home, Siwans are increasingly keeping part of it as a cool and comfortable place to live in hot weather. The impact on tourism also seems to have been appreciated. One woman who sells handicrafts from her spacious mud-built house, told me that, for the time being, she and her husband prefer not to exchange their traditional home for a modern house because foreigners are interested in visiting it.

6 The World of Women

The life of a Siwan woman revolves around her home, her children, and the comfort of her husband. Almost all her private and social life takes place in the home. Unlike her husband, she does not spend time outside working, shopping, or meeting friends, much less encountering strangers. She will also perform her religious devotions at home while he goes with other men to the mosque. Siwan women receive visits from neighbors and relatives at home, where the latest news is discussed and daily concerns are aired. It is common, in the afternoon, to visit relatives or neighbors, on foot or by *carusa* or *careta*, or now by tuktuk, always returning by sunset. Visiting can take up a lot of a woman's time, but it is counted on for company and support. It is a custom and an obligation to offer congratulations on the occasions of a birth or a marriage. A woman will be visited after she has been in hospital, or returns from seeing a doctor in Marsa Matrouh or Alexandria. A mother will receive congratulatory visits when a son finishes his education in one of these places, is about to join the army, or returns to Siwa after completing his compulsory military service. A woman will not usually visit those who have failed to visit her on such occasions.

When a Siwan woman prepares to go out visiting, she puts on a 'best' dress and headshawl (*shal*). Over her dress she pulls on a voluminous silky black dress with an embroidered square collar. Next she ties a black face-

veil over her headshawl. She then draws on the *tarfutet*, a large blue-and-white-checked cotton shawl that has been woven for the Siwans for centuries in the village of Kerdassa, on the edge of Cairo. When the woman arrives at her destination, she flips back her veil over her headshawl, or deftly pleats it on the top of her head, giving the impression of an elegant toque, though fashions change every day in the oasis.

Siwans (especially young married women) began to wear a black Islamic face veil under the *tarfutet* after the new road from Marsa Matrouh was built. Traditionally, the women would draw the *tarfutet* across the face and hold it in the mouth leaving only one eye uncovered when they passed men in the street. They seem to see the new veiling as a commitment to modesty within all the social upheavals of rapidly changing times. On a more practical note, some say that the veil allows them to see more easily, and has the advantage that it frees their hands to carry things, as opposed to clutching the *tarfutet* over the face in the increasingly busy streets.

35. Visiting by donkey cart.

36. A mother and daughter on their way to a wedding. *Vincent Battesti, Feb. 2006.*

A woman's attire expresses her modesty and allegiance to her community. This is not to say that the Siwan women are resistant to the allure of modern living—they are constantly adapting old ideas to new. Even the older generation, living in the extended family and surrounded by new situations, make concessions to change. However, they are sad to see elements of their Berber heritage slipping away, and still value old customs and disapprove of the desire of some of the young to dress and wear makeup like the women they see in Egyptian television serials. By and large, girls respect the wishes of their elders, but they are exposed to modern influences through television and the internet. Some now leave the home to work in local factories where dates are washed, dried, and packed into boxes, or where olives are processed. Others find employment in workshops that produce carpets, embroideries, or rugs and tapestries to sell from a government shop in Siwa; some are employed in an atelier where high-quality embroidery is produced for the local and overseas market. However, such periods of employment are temporary. The girls who work in these factories and workshops are all single, and once they are married their working and social lives will be confined to the domestic sphere. It is the responsibility of the husband to go out to work and provide for the family.

In Siwa, it is the women who are the guardians of tradition and custom, and it is women who have been responsible for the survival of the Siwan language. The men, through their close contacts with the Awlad Ali Bedouin, through trading or temporary migration, have long understood and spoken Arabic, and many men are now also fluent in English and may speak some French and German as a result of their involvement in the tourist industry. The women speak Siwi with their children and friends but Arabic words and phrases are entering the language as a result of the arrival of Arabic-language television since the mid-1980s, and the recent influx of Arabic-speaking families from other parts of Egypt drawn by job opportunities in agriculture and tourism. Likewise, children are taught in Arabic in school, which is regarded as essential to their future, but Siwans believe it is also important to preserve their Berber language. Many women and girls are taking advantage of a government literacy program that offers free Arabic and mathematics lessons taught by local girls who have been specially trained. They can thus conveniently attend classes in the home of a neighbor.

Marriage

All Siwan girls are expected to marry, usually around the age of seventeen, or even sixteen, but girls who are completing high school in Siwa now delay marriage until they are eighteen. The man will typically be a few years older because he needs time to accumulate the *mahr*, or marriage payment. The age difference, and the fact that he is more experienced in the world, also make it more likely that the wife will fulfill the expectation that she will respect him and be obedient. Marriage in Siwa is patrilocal. On the day she marries, a girl moves from her home to live with her husband and his parents, brothers and sisters, and sisters-in-law. From then on the only men she will be seen by and speak to are her and her husband's closest male relatives. In company, her husband will never mention her name or speak of her to other men.

Though Islam permits a man to have up to four wives, in Siwa the tradition is to have only one. Monogamy enhances family solidarity and harmony. In the past, divorce and remarriage was common but, reflecting trends in other parts of the country, Siwan marriages are now more stable and permanent. If a couple does divorce, the wife will return to live with her parents (or an elder brother), taking with her jewelry and other property that was purchased with the marriage payment. If the woman has no grounds for divorce or if she rejects her husband early in the marriage, he will be entitled to keep the *mahr*. He will soon remarry and she also is expected to marry again. After any divorce the former husband must provide for the children, who will live with their mother until a girl is about twelve years old and a boy about nine. They will then go to join his household.

If a woman's husband dies, unless they owned their own home, she will leave the home of her parents-in-law to return to her parents with the children. She will then be expected to remarry after a period of mourning. Her new husband may have his own children and is not obliged to care for hers, thus her children may then live with their maternal or paternal grandparents.

Domestic duties

Caring for her children, cleaning the house, laundering clothes, preparing meals, and baking bread are important female responsibilities. Mothers train their young daughters to do housework and care for a baby or toddler so that when they marry they will know how to carry out their household duties efficiently. Training a young girl to do housework may also involve play-work. For example, Fathi Malim says that after Eid al-Adha, when there is spare meat in the house, mothers will give their daughters meat and rice so that they can practice cooking. They are expected to build a mud stove, make a wood fire, and prepare a meal on their own.[31]

It is common also to see young girls making baskets or doing embroidery, either together or under the supervision of their mothers, to sell in the souq. Embroidery remains a highly valued and well-established skill. It is the custom for a girl to begin to sew *(yizme)* from the age of seven. She will learn from her mother the shapes and names of the Siwan motifs, as well as the different embroidery stitches. By fifteen, she will be experienced and proficient in embroidery and she may also know how to weave baskets evenly and get a good shape.

Food and shopping

A married woman must rely on the men in her family to do the shopping, but there are a few small grocery outlets she can frequent. These are located within ordinary homes, without an open frontage, and are managed and patronized by women. In one, a customer can buy staple foodstuffs on account and pay after the harvest. This is common practice in the oasis. If a woman finds it difficult to put together the money for food, the shopkeeper will accept her embroidery to sell. This kind of shop also supplies hanks of silky pale green thread to embroider cloth or decorate baskets, and chemical dyes to color the thread and the palm leaves which are used to embellish the baskets.

Food For Everyday and Celebration

Dates, olives, pumpkin, okra, tomatoes, onions, horseradish, and garlic are grown in the oasis, and fruits include figs, apricots, and pomegranates. Fruit and vegetables are also imported from Alexandria and Marsa Matrouh. Grains, which are very important in the diet, come from North America and Europe. Meat may be mutton, goat, camel, chicken, and small birds. From these ingredients, the women prepare local and national dishes for the family and for celebrations. Typical dishes are *mulukhiya*, a soup Egyptians make from the leaves of the Jew's mallow plant which grows well in Siwa, a local variety of *shakshouka* (a vegetable and egg ragout prepared across North Africa), and a local broth called *makhmakh* which includes the spinach-like leaves of the strong-tasting purslane plant. Dates are used in a variety of ways such as mixed with bread and olive oil; cooked with eggs and olive oil; and cooked with flour, oil, and water to make *taglentenu*. Dates eaten with olive oil are said by the older generation of

Siwans to form a particularly delicious and healthy meal. Dates will accompany every meal and snack.

Perhaps because the Siwans have traditionally worked hard, they are accustomed to eating at frequent intervals during the day. The first meal, *fitur* (breakfast), is taken between 7:00 and 8:00 a.m. and commonly consists of cheese, falafel, bread, and stewed dried broad beans, called *fuul*. This is followed by *dahwera*, between 10:00 and 11:00 a.m., which might include soup, beans, milk, and a salad vegetable like tomatoes. The main meal, *ghada*, is at about 1:00 p.m. This normally consists of pasta, a salad or cooked vegetable dish, and olives. Meat also may be served. At 5:00 p.m. there is *asriya*, comprising a light snack such as a salad vegetable like cucumber, with peanuts. At 7:00 p.m. comes another light meal called *asha*, followed by a final snack at 11:00 p.m.

The family customarily eats together. In the large extended family, however, men and women may eat separately, the men first. Family members take their meals sitting on a kilim, a palm, or a patterned plastic mat around a tray on which the dishes are placed. They help themselves from a common dish and tear off small pieces of fresh bread to scoop up the food. After meals, two cups of strong, very sweet green tea are taken, often with mint. Tea drinking in Siwa follows a ritual in which the first glass is returned to the pot before it is poured out for everyone. Coffee, which was disapproved of by the Senoussis, is not drunk much in Siwa.

Siwans are hospitable and welcoming, and whether rich or poor, they are generous hosts. A female guest will eat with the women and a male with the men in a separate room. The presentation of food as well as the taste is important, and the platter of salad vegetables straight from the market is always fresh and bright.

Baking Bread

Baking bread for the family two or three times a week is an important task for a Siwan woman. This is done in a mud oven, the *tabint*, in the open at the back of the house, although a gas-fueled bread oven may be used indoors, especially in the winter or if a woman is old or ill. The whole bread-making process is made easier when two neighbors join forces as they often do, one taking care of the fire and the other putting the bread in the oven. When a Siwan friend called Naama makes bread, it is not unusual to find her measuring out five kilos of flour for one bread-making session, even though she must repeat the process in three days' time. Naama is baking for the large extended family, and fresh bread is an important part of every meal. She kneads the dough she has made from flour, salt, yeast, and water, divides it, and rolls it into balls. She then flattens the balls with the palm of her hand, places them on a tray, covers them with a cloth, and leaves them to rise. When the mud oven is hot she stokes the fire with an olive stick, and places the first batch inside the oven. She flips the rounds over with a palm frond and, when the bread is ready, transfers it on the frond from the oven to a tray.

Food for celebrations

Festive occasions are marked by the production of a variety of special sweet and savory dishes that the women make together. Describing the preparations for Eid al-Fitr, Muhammad Ibrahim Moussa says,

> During the last week of Ramadan, all the women in the family gather—to help make the cookies that will be served on Eid Al Fitr . . . . *Menina* are only made in Siwa. Dough, made from flour, oil, eggs and sugar, is pressed flat and then cut into thick squares the size of a child's hand. Then traditional designs, many of which are also used as motifs in henna, are etched onto the cookie with a knife.[32]

Dates symbolize the fertility of the bride and groom and they are included in many dishes made for a wedding, such as date bread which will be served sliced, and a dessert called *libsees* that consists just of crushed dates is provided in little plastic containers or in the hand.

A dish made with nutritious crushed wheat and tomatoes, onions, and offal, called *dishish*, is served on the last day of a wedding, which is also popularly known as *youm al-dishish*. When the bride and her guests have eaten it, the festivities have concluded and everybody goes home.

Childbirth is also an occasion for special foods. Before the event, a kind of dry bread called *tankutat*, made with the herb fenugreek, is prepared. Shortly before a Siwan friend's baby was born, I was shown the small pieces piled high against a wall in a room of the house. In the first three days after the birth they would be distributed among the neighbors. Her whole family would enjoy a dish called *tankutat nhilba* for which the pieces of bread are mixed with hot water, sugar, and butter. The new mother would have it with honey. Fenugreek *(hilba)* has a long history in Egypt and is believed to be good for mother's milk. The ancient Egyptians used it to bring on childbirth. During the first seven days after the birth, the Siwan mother rests in bed and is given a lot of attention. She is given nourishing foods such as chicken soup, macaroni cooked in a fenugreek stock with butter, liver, rice, and perhaps a whole chicken for herself.

The birth ceremony *(seboua)*, which takes place seven days after the birth, is also marked by the serving of special foods. Barley, beans, dates, and rice, all of which have symbolized fertility since ancient times, are included in the dishes. A sheep will be sacrificed if the family can afford this. Fish is also significant because of the story the Siwans tell about the birth of their patron saint Sidi Suleiman. His mother was apparently unable to give birth, in great discomfort, and had a tremendous craving for fish. Fish was unobtainable in the oasis, but miraculously a bird flew through the window bringing a fish, which was cooked and eaten without delay. As soon as Sidi Suleiman's mother had eaten it, he was born. Salted fish thus became a food to give to pregnant women, and to serve at certain celebrations.

Eids

Special times in the lives of the people of Siwa are the *eids*. These are regular festivals or feasts which take place throughout the year, some having universal Islamic significance, others being purely local. Eid al-Fitr and Eid al-Adha are two major religious festivals celebrated throughout the Muslim world according to the lunar Islamic calendar. The first follows Ramadan, the most significant of months, a period of piety and abstinence from food, liquids, sex, and smoking, from the first light of dawn until sunset. It is the job of the town crier, called in Siwa the *boab*, to wake the people at about 3:00 a.m. by beating his drum so as to notify them that it is time to eat the *suhour*, a meal taken before dawn prayers and the beginning of a new day of fasting. Eid al-Fitr marks the end of the fast of Ramadan and begins after morning prayers in the mosque when the family eats together a special breakfast *(fitur)* of rice, meat, and vegetables. There follows a day of rejoicing where, wearing their best clothes, Siwans jump onto their donkey carts and go off to visit friends and relations.

Eid al-Adha, or the Feast of Sacrifice, takes place at the end of the Hajj, the pilgrimage month, and is a major festival for which Muslims everywhere buy sheep to sacrifice in commemoration of Ibrahim's readiness to sacrifice his son Ismail, and his victory over the devil. All over Siwa special feasts take place over a period of four days. On the first, the skin of the sheep, together with its liver, heart, and kidney, are cooked in oil and eaten; and on the second, the legs, head, and stomach are eaten. It is the Islamic duty of wealthier members of the community to share their meat with the poor. Until a couple of decades ago the meat was preserved in salt so it could be eaten over a long period, and the collection of blocks of the salt from nearby lakes by the men on their donkey carts was a feature of the Siwan celebration. Today the advent of the refrigerator means that the meat can be kept without the need for salt, but nevertheless salt is still collected and cut by the men, then milled by the women for everyday use.

In Siwa, there are three *eid*s of purely local significance. The first is Eid al-Siyaha, an annual feast that spans three days of the autumn full moon. It is celebrated by men, children, and unmarried girls with their fathers in an encampment on the slopes of the mountain of Dakrour. The women do not take part in that aspect of the *eid*, but they do prepare special food and gather in the homes of relatives to enjoy a relaxing time with other women.

Describing the feast, Fathi Malim explains that the meat of camels, cows, and sheep is cooked, cut up, and "skewered on palm tree thorns. . . . Once the food is ready, the cooks balance the dishes on their heads and run down the mountain to the groups of people assembled in circles on the floor."[33] The communities of the East and West share the feast served on

38. The tomb of Sidi Suleiman attached to the new mosque, with an old mosque in the foreground (1930s). *Royal Geographical Society.*

large trays, in a mood of harmony, and during a religious ritual at night "any problems or disputes are reconciled."[34]

The second is Eid al-Ashur, held during Muharram, the first month of the Islamic year. In the past, this festival was principally for children, who would make frames of palm fronds decorated with oranges, nuts, sweets, and cookies and parade them through the streets. The frames made by boys were roughly in the shape of a cross; those by the girls like a square. Palm branches played a prominent and dramatic role in the festivities. Long branches were cut down in the date gardens, brought home on donkey carts, and placed on the roofs of houses where there were children. When it was dark, the branches were actually set alight using torches soaked in oil. The whole town was illuminated as children's songs echoed around the town. However, rest assured, this aspect of the ceremony has long since been abandoned.

The third special holiday is the birthday, or *moulid*, of Siwa's patron saint Sidi Suleiman, which takes place after the corn harvest. Siwans bring food and gather to eat together by the Saint's tomb, which is attached to the mosque in the town square. In the evening, a Sufi group called Darawish (who, on Thursday nights, can regularly be heard drumming and chanting their rituals at the tomb) perform their ceremonies. The festival used to be a more elaborate event, and for days preparations were visible to all. The tomb of the saint was whitewashed, the springs were cleaned, houses swept, and carpets and mats beaten and hung from roofs and windows to air out. The rich sheikhs slaughtered sheep and as many as three or four camels, and distributed meat among the poor. After the feast families went into the streets to visit friends and relations, and watched the sheikhs in colorful silk robes, riding their donkeys through the town. At dusk, the men processed in long lines to visit the tomb of Sidi Suleiman, which was lit with lanterns and candles. Later, they assembled in the square, making circles, and dancing *zikr*s (religious dances). Describing the scene, Belgrave says,

> Numbers of women squat on the outskirts of the crowd, huddled in their dark robes, hardly visible, except when the moon gleams on their silver ornaments and pale white faces. Some of them are burning incense in little earthenware braziers, and occasionally one of them creeps up to the white tomb and kisses the wall. . . . The sheikhs walk slowly about from group to group, each followed by a little knot of men-servants carrying carpets and cushions.[35]

39. The tomb of Sidi
Suleiman: a recent
interior view.

The *eids* are always times of relaxation and enjoyment. The streets fill with donkey carts taking families to visit their relations and friends, children play out in their new clothes, and older girls link arms and walk in the town. Girls will have painted henna patterns on their hands, or had their friends do it for them. Some wear traditional bead necklaces. For weeks the women will have been planning their new clothes for the festivities, and many will have paid a visit to the dressmaker with the fabrics they have chosen. They typically spend 500 to 700 Egyptian pounds on a dress. The men will have bought clothes for themselves and their sons in the souq, or during a visit to Marsa Matrouh or Alexandria.

Visiting is particularly important during an *eid*. The women and their daughters and daughters-in-law will have prepared the guest room, swept it with a broom cut from palms, unrolled an oriental carpet if they have one, and placed bowls filled with peanuts, chickpeas, and sweets on a low table for visitors to enjoy. Wealthy households will have cut down a date palm, usually a weak male, for its delicious white heart, known as *gumar*. It is presented on a tray, and pieces are carved off and given to all visitors.

Birth and Death
Death

Men and women have special roles at the time of a death. When a Siwan dies he or she must be buried in one of the cemeteries in the East or the West. If the death occurred in the night, the burial will be early the next morning. If the death occurred during the day, the burial will take place before sunset. The whole town is informed of a death by the town crier, who passes each house giving details of the funeral, the time, and the name of the cemetery. He does not give the name of the deceased. The inhabitants must themselves inquire after who has died.

Close female relatives then dress in black and remove their jewelry. Relatives and neighbors clean and prepare the house and make space for people who will soon arrive from all directions. They bake bread and clean the rice that will be served after the funeral. They may bake traditional *menina* cookies, especially if the deceased is an old person, to celebrate a long and propitious life. The midwife traditionally helps in organizing the funeral, and she provides her services free of charge. The men, dressed in white, lay a carpet outside the mosque, where they will gather to eat a meal together after the funeral. The body of the deceased is ritually washed five times. If it is a woman, there are women in the community who will wash the body; if a man, men will perform this function.

Most of the town makes its way to the house to offer condolences to the family. The women crowd into the house, and sit in absolute silence, while the men remain outside. Women mourners dressed in black stay behind when the men carry the body on the bier to the cemetery. They stand up when the body is carried out of the house. Describing a funeral in 1973 Ahmed Fakhry wrote that,

> (t)he women utter very loud cries, tear their clothes, beat their breasts, throw dust over their heads and, sometimes, smear their faces with mud or some blue grit. . . . With their hair plaited in a number of small tresses and their exaggerated signs of grief, they present a living picture of Ancient Egyptian women represented on the funeral scenes on the walls of the ancient tombs.[36]

40. Hands embroidered on a child's bonnet.

At the cemetery, the body, wrapped in its shrouds, is lowered into the deep grave. Logs are placed on top; and then earth, and small stones. Palm fronds are strewn over. A white stone is placed on a woman's grave, and two on a man's. In the past, incense was burnt, and pots were placed on the grave to ward off evil spirits.

Birth

A birth is a significant and very desirable event that will be immediately announced to neighbors and relatives. Traditionally a baby was born in the home and delivered by the local midwife who was conversant with all the traditions surrounding birth, while today a baby will more likely be born in the local hospital under the care of doctors. One person, who may be the mother or sister of the new mother, takes care of her and the baby throughout the first week after the birth. Traditionally, she would swaddle the child, folding and wrapping two fine white cloths, one for the head and neck, and the other for the lower body, to bind the arms firmly to the body. Swaddling prevented any scratching and kept the child warm. There is a local belief that the practice helped make the person strong and secure in the future. The baby's eyes would also be outlined with soft black kohl powder as a medicinal measure. Some people say that this made the eyes look very large. It may have been a way to repel the envious gaze because babies are believed to be vulnerable to the evil eye.

In the week before the birth ceremony (*seboua*) it was a custom not to tell the relatives and neighbors who visited the family whether the newborn was male or female. There were, however, special ways of imparting the information. It was not uncommon, when it was a boy, for his grandmother to say to visitors, "We have *afesh*," a term which was applied to newborn boys, and show her delight. If she did not say *afesh* visitors would know it was a girl and they would not ask. Only close relatives might do so. On the other hand, she might say, "We have *afesha*," deliberately obscuring their good fortune to avoid the damaging effects of the envious gaze. *Afesh* and *afesha* in fact mean 'dirty little thing,' a term of endearment.

On the seventh day following the birth, the midwife *(takadumt)* took the leading part in the *seboua*. Pots made by the women potters were used and had special significance. Bettina Leopoldo, who spent many winters in Siwa, describes a birth ceremony for twins in the 1980s. It begins with the midwife lighting seven candles and an incense burner containing olive-tree twigs and a special unguent *(jowee)* made from 'seven secret ingredients.' After sipping water from a clay cup *(makalay)* filled from a clay jar *(ajrang)*, she takes the babies from the mother. From a bowl of henna she

41. An incense burner.

uses her finger to make five marks on each baby's forehead, and one mark on the inside of each hand. These marks are called tassabut. During this time she is humming and repeating their names for the first time. . . . This singing is called ajhow, and will keep away evil spirits. The women now start to hum with her, reciting also from the Koran. The whole atmosphere becomes very thick. The room is full of smoke, the pervading smell of the incense, and the babies' names are chanted very loud.[37]

These days, the baby is specially dressed in new white clothes for the birth ceremony. He or she will be ritually incorporated into the family and Muslim community. A Muslim name will have been chosen (and in the past, a Berber name might have been given also). In the birth ceremony, protection is an important theme, and prayers of thanks to God are offered for the safe delivery of the child and the safety of the mother.

If the baby is a girl, on the seventh day, her ears may be pierced with little 21-karat gold earrings. Traditionally the midwife did this using a needle *(teezignit)* and thread. The thread stayed in place until it healed.

The Henna Arts

Red henna is applied to the skin in ceremonies that mark important phases of life. During the birth ceremony and the circumcision of a boy, the babies are daubed with red paste. For Ramadan and *eid*s, and for the return of the pilgrims from Mecca, girls and women decorate their skin with henna patterns. On the eve of a wedding, there is an important ceremony, called *leilat al-henna*—the henna night—when young unmarried girls use henna to paint patterns on the bride's hands, arms, legs, and feet. The henna arts are predominately the province of girls and married women in Siwa, although a bridegroom and male guests under the age of thirty may also decorate the palms of their hands. As well as ornamenting the body, henna—so Siwans say—makes people smile and be happy. It is believed to purify, to bring good luck, and to protect against the evil eye. Its powers to deflect evil probably lie behind the old Arab proverb, "If I don't speak truth I won't present my hand for henna,"[38] but if there are problems in the family, or if someone is in hospital, henna will not be used.

Red henna paste is made from the crushed leaves of the henna plant *(lawsonia inermis)*, with Egypt, India, and Sudan as major suppliers. Egypt has been a producer since earliest times. Ancient Egyptian mummies have been discovered with red nails and hair and it is thought that henna may have been used by them. In the first century, Dioscorides praised the henna grown at Canopus in the Delta.

All the girls in Siwa are adept at doing the henna, either painting one another's skin or doing their own. There are accomplished and well-known henna artists in the community but over the years, their role has changed. At the beginning of the twentieth century, when girls married very young, the task of painting the patterns on the bride's skin was entrusted only to a mature woman who was the wedding specialist. Later it became customary for young married women to do it, and now it is the role of unmarried girls.

Whatever the occasion on which henna is to be used, the henna artist's first task is to prepare the paste by mixing the powdered henna with hot brewed tea. Then, using a small stick, like a toothpick, she applies it to the skin with short strokes, cleanly removing any smudges of the thick paste as she proceeds. She first paints a large motif, such as a star, on the center of the palm of the hand, which will relate to the patterns she then

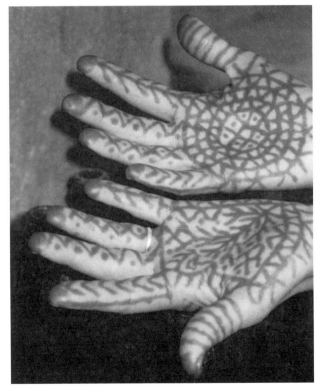

42. Typical Siwan henna designs.

paints over the rest of the palm, along the fingers and thumb, and over the front of the hand. Space is an important element of her design. The raised lines of henna paste resemble a tracery of black lace over the skin. The patterns are linear foliate, floral, and geometric, all conforming to the notion that Islam prohibits the representation of human and animal forms. Some of the designs are linked to patterns engraved on Siwan jewelry and embroideries. The henna patterns have evolved over the years from simpler patterns, which some old people say were once just lines and dots. Girls and young women are now looking further afield for ideas, such as henna designs from Pakistan and India. After several hours, the dried paste is removed with lukewarm water, leaving behind red patterns that seem now to be part of the skin. The design will last for about two weeks; whenever the hands are washed the designs will fade a little more.

Decorating their skin with elaborate henna patterns is principally done by the young. Older women restrict themselves to staining the soles of their feet, their fingertips, and palms by submerging these parts to be stained in paste until they emerge the color of ripe dates. They then make bold stripes across their fingers or palms using any straight edge or everyday object that is to hand. Horriya, for example, showed me how she could take a glass bowl with a scalloped edge to cut through the damp henna with which she had coated the palm of her hand, to make a pattern of diagonal lines. It was a chilly February afternoon, and we were sitting with her daughters Zeinab and Muna in their garden, around a crackling fire they had made with olive branches. It was the week after Eid al-Adha, and they had painted one another's hands with beautiful designs for the festival. Zeinab painted traditional patterns over my palms that afternoon, resting her right hand on her left to keep it steady. About three hours later, after the henna was finished and we had had tea, we removed the dried paste with lukewarm water.

These days girls and young women also use stencils to do the henna, either making their own or buying intricately cut sheets from the souq made by particularly talented Siwan girls, or from beauty salons in Marsa Matrouh. A large stencil will include designs to decorate the hands, legs, and feet. The stencils are laid onto the skin and the henna is used to fill in the cut-outs. This new method is popular among young girls in Siwa now because of its speed and the attractive images it produces on the skin. Older women are not so keen, and say that the traditional art, in which patterns are drawn free-hand, and which demands a higher level of technical and artistic ability, is so much more rewarding.

43. A stencil sheet comprising henna strips for the palm, the back of the hand, the fingers and thumbs, and the legs and feet from Marsa Matrouh.

Cosmetics

Except for kohl, or in Siwi *tasalt*, to outline the eyes, it is not the custom for Siwan women to use cosmetics on the face, and young unmarried girls wear neither kohl nor scent. Today a few of the older girls will wear a little makeup on special occasions, but though it is hardly visible, others will be critical, saying it is better to be natural and pretty. It would not be surprising if a girl, paying a visit to Marsa Matrouh or Alexandria with her family, was tempted by the range of cosmetics displayed in the windows of the beauty shops. Nevertheless, a new trend has reached Siwa which follows the Egyptian custom for brides to be professionally made up and their hair styled. Some Siwan brides are now being adorned in this way with their hair arranged high under their veil.

Hairstyles

In the past Siwan women wore an elegant plaited hairdo known as the *tcoset*. Its most distinctive features were the arrangement of braids at the front that crossed over the forehead, and a couple of plaits that hung over each cheek. The *tcoset* was made with thirty-three braids from ninety-nine strands symbolizing the ninety-nine epithets of God.

The style, which was still being worn when I visited the oasis in the mid-1980s, was widespread within Siwa though it was not universal. Older people remember that a different coiffure for married women, called *tirkirt*, was worn by some women into the 1950s. It was sculptural and dramatic, projecting out at the back of the head and exaggerating its shape.

There are photos taken in the first half of the twentieth century that show little girls with their heads shaved except for sidelocks and a lock of hair on the crown, and of older girls with their heads completely shaved, which took place at about nine years of age. The hair was allowed to grow back, and was then worn in many braids that fell to the shoulders and formed a straight fringe over the eyes. This style, called *cushit*, resembled the hairstyle and wigs that can be seen being worn by Ancient Egyptians in wall paintings and reliefs. In more recent times a simpler plaited style, called *tederbolain*, came into fashion. The hair was drawn off the forehead and plaited in a series of braids close to the head to the hairline and plaited on to hang loose around the shoulders, and the ends tied with silk thread.

Braided hairstyles can still be seen in Siwa, but the elaborate traditional coiffures are just a memory now. Women and girls today prefer simpler styles. Long hair is commonly worn in two plaits called *defira*, though a chignon is fashionable. Long, shiny, and well-cared-for hair is regarded as a sign of beauty and good health. Older women are less concerned with fashion, and often tidy their shortish hair into several plaits.

Yesterday

7 Motifs and Magic

Ornamentation is second nature to the Siwans. Succeeding generations have decorated their jewelry and clothes with patterns that are repeated throughout their handicrafts. These designs are decorative but also reflect local concerns and confer good fortune and ancestral wellbeing. The embroidered costume and silver ornaments first worn by a young bride are embellished with motifs and materials that are thought to assist her fertility and protect her from the evil eye. Indeed, the 'evil eye' is important to any study of the traditional arts of North Africa because of the large variety of decorative symbols it generates.

Belief in the 'eye'—in Arabic *ayn*—is a system of thought which attributes ill-fortune, illness, or other calamities to the harmful, malicious, or involuntary gaze of another person and not to bad luck or accident. People may become suspects if they possess physical or social defects like having a squint, or being an infertile woman. Another person's success or good looks are believed to be enough to provoke someone who is envious to cast the eye; thus the instinct of a prosperous North African farmer whose date trees become diseased, a bride who does not conceive, a new mother whose breasts dry up, or a woman who becomes ill after wearing a large amount of precious jewelry at a social gathering, is to see themselves as being victims.

Throughout the Mediterranean people have traditionally tried to protect themselves from the eye by taking preventative measures. These include gestures with the hand; fumigating with incense; practices which involve salt or water; and uttering incantations. People also wear amulets—small ornaments that possess a magical power against evil. Amuletic devices such as these are said to be prophylactic against the evil eye. The Arabic word for amulet is *hijab*. The verb *hajaba* means to veil, to screen, or to conceal, suggesting that an amulet will keep the wearer safe from harm.

Like other Berber groups across North Africa, Siwans believe that silver itself has amuletic qualities, and they attribute many blessings and magical powers to the metal. Silver is associated with goodness, and is prized for its healing properties and as a defense against evil. Its highly reflective surface will surely deflect the first glance of the evil eye, which is thought to be its most dangerous. Siwans use a special word, *twetwat*, to describe the shine of materials such as silver and gold, mirror, and glass.

Forms that represent sharp objects, and shapes with sharp corners that can pierce, also are incorporated into North African jewelry and textiles and perform a defensive function. Among the time-honored motifs that Siwan women embroider over their traditional wedding tunics and headshawls are the sword, scissors, garden knife, comb, crescent, and seal. The motif of the seal, *khatem*, which incorporates triangles, decorates the front neckline of the wedding tunics and the ankle cuffs of the trousers that are worn underneath. In many regions of the world it was thought evil spirits could enter openings of the body and of clothing. We also find an embroidered seal motif positioned at the nape of the neck of the wedding tunic, another vulnerable part of the body.

The seal was displayed at ceremonies relating to rites of passage such as marriage and circumcision and, as well as being a protective symbol, it was a mark of the person's new role in the community. It decorated one side of the special paper that was placed on a Siwan boy's head after his hair had been shaved in a circumcision rite, while on the other side of the paper there were crescents. The designs were drawn by a *fikh*, a magician who wrote amulets. For a week after the circumcision, the boy, who would be about seven years old, wore the paper pinned to the top of his cap as a protection against the evil eye. After this, the paper was cut into strips. In the 1920s, Cline was told that these strips of paper were worn by the women, pinned to their hair under the headshawl, "to ensure for them the love of their husbands."[39] Ibrahim, who was in his mid-seventies, told me that this paper was red or green and there were verses from the Qur'an written on it.

The embroidered square collar that enriches the married woman's traditional wide *akbir nwasa* dress incorporates a tightly coiled motif that was probably designed to have a protective function. A winding pattern has been used in places across the globe to engage, ensnare, or ward off a hostile spirit or envious glance. The open space above the motif emphasizes and draws attention to it.

Throughout North Africa, movement, sound, smell, and color have also been used to ward off evil forces by diverting attention to the swish of fringes, tassels, and chains. The tinkle of bells and the aroma of products taken from the natural environment, such as garlic and cumin, also perform this function. The red henna that women paint on their hands and feet forms part of this system of ornamentation and provides a protective and healing screen for the body. People try to shield themselves from the evil eye by decorating their houses, shops, and vehicles with protective signs and amulets. They position them where they can easily be seen such as on house walls and above doorways to avert it from the entrance to the house. Most Siwan springs, gardens, and houses were once so protected. When I first went to stay in Siwa in 1999, there were only a few prophylactic devices remaining: the skull of a donkey set high on a pole in a palm garden and a dead bustard nailed over the garden entrance to a house to repel the malevolent glance; ram's horns set into the mud wall of a house; blue hands painted on the wall of another house; and a bright red rag fastened to a donkey's neck. Many people still painted dot-in-a-circle motifs on their donkey carts or carriages, which appears to have had a protective function. In the last few years this traditional motif has been replaced by designs with no obvious protective function, though the back of a *careta* or *carusa* occasionally displays a realistic depiction of two eyes, or two circles or rosettes. The owner of a car or truck protects it by hanging amulets around the windshield and at the back. In the past, the owner of a truck might burn incense under it before driving it out through the town, to protect the vehicle and its occupants from the envious gaze.

44. Donkey carts decorated with protective symbols.

The Eye

A realistic image of an eye or an abstract representation of one is clearly the most effective way to counteract the evil eye. Geometric shapes like diamonds, circles, squares, and oblongs, and figures such as eight-pointed stars and rosettes, have all been used to represent the eye. A dot-in-a-circle motif has been used for thousands of years, painted on or carved into materials such as stone, shell, ivory, wood, and metal. This symbol was drawn on the ground by Tuareg potters before they fired their pots.[40] In Siwa, bright, round mother-of-pearl (*sadaf*) buttons are also an important protective element in the decoration of garments, leather jewelry, costume accessories, and baskets that hold goods and produce. Other shiny objects like cowrie shells (*agabez*) and sequins have similar protective qualities and are used with the buttons to embellish the Siwan bride's wedding costume. In Siwa, mother-of-pearl buttons are given the name *tutintfukt* ('eye of the sun') because they seem to reflect the sun's intense white light. In different contexts and regions of the world, mother-of-pearl shapes and other shiny sequins covering the surfaces of garments have been described as making a protective barrier of light over the body.

For thousands of years people have traded and worn shiny eye-like beads. In the Middle East, blue or blue-green beads, in particular, and bright red or yellow beads were thought to have the power to cast back the ill-intended look on the beholder. 'Eye beads,' made from a variety of materials such as stone, faience, glass, and in recent years, plastic, were decorated with both naturally occurring and fabricated eye motifs that were thought to invest them with significant magical power.

In Siwa, cowrie shells are treasured for their beautiful iridescence, and women thread them into a traditional necklace that is worn by a bride. These light and durable little shells are used also to decorate traditional wedding dresses and headshawls. The cowrie, which resembles a half-closed eye, is used throughout Africa and the Middle East for protection. It also serves as a fertility symbol through its resemblance to the female genitalia. For centuries, tiny cowries were transported in large quantities from the Indian Ocean, and distributed along the camel routes. The *cypraea moneta*, in particular, was used as a form of currency in Africa.

The Hand

Throughout North Africa the hand is a symbol of power and protection. Blue or red hands painted on the walls of a house, a red plastic hand suspended above the entrance to a shop, or a little silver or gold hand worn on a necklace will provide protection from the evil eye. In Siwa, a beaded image of the hand is stitched to a bride's wedding dress and headshawl, and the hand recurs repeatedly among the tiny embroidered motifs that embellish these garments.

In North Africa the number five *(khamsa)* also possesses a magical value against the evil eye. Motifs with five elements are frequently used to decorate jewelry and textiles: a cross, or a flower with four petals plus its center, consists of five parts. If the fives are multiplied by two or more the motif gains power. In Siwa a star with eight points or an equivalent rosette are often used to decorate silver jewelry and embroidery. The hand itself, with its five fingers, is called *khamsa* and, in Siwan embroidery, a motif which depicts two hands linked together is called *khamsa wa khamesa*, 'five and five.' When hands are joined to the arms of a cross motif (called *tarust*, which means 'bride') the new motif is called *tarust we khamesa*. Fives are frequently picked out with different colored threads, for instance for the multiple spokes of a solar motif.

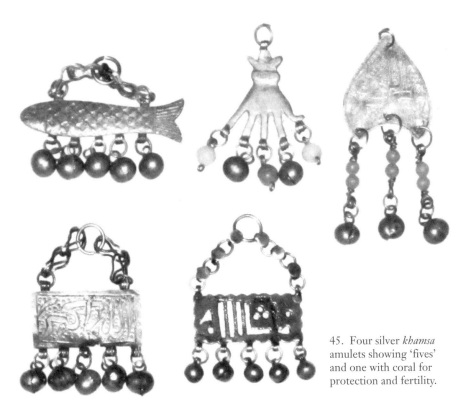

45. Four silver *khamsa* amulets showing 'fives' and one with coral for protection and fertility.

Amulets

Individuals passing through rites of passage, such as birth, marriage, and circumcision, were believed to be susceptible to the envious gaze and consequently needed to be well protected against it. In Siwa, a local *fikh* or sheikh would give advice about the choice of personal amulets. These might be appropriate Qur'anic verses, or magical signs, written on paper; or silver pendant plaques with religious inscriptions such as *mashaallah* ('as God wills') or *Ayat al-Kursi* (the Throne Verse from the Qur'an). Amulets could also be acquired from the *attar* who traveled along the camel routes with his supplies of herbs, homeopathic medicines, beads, and trinkets that were believed to contain magical properties. One *fikh* in Siwa told me that for a bride he would choose a *gingilt* (a little silver heart-shaped amulet) set with a blue or green stone to link through her earring; a silver *khamsa* to tie to a braid of her hair; or he would provide a *hijab* comprising a piece of paper on which he wrote verses from the Qur'an—a widely used defense, particularly for brides and babies. The *suras*, chapters, 113 and 114 that begin: *Say I take refuge with the Lord of the Dawn* and *I seek refuge with the Lord of men, the King of mankind* are the most effective against the evil eye. The paper would be put into a small leather bag and might be pinned to a garment, or placed among the clothes in a bride's red marriage chest.

The following story about a necklace of written amulets was told to me by Ibrahim.

My father always wore seven amulets around his neck, but he was deprived of his good fortune and power when, on a visit to Khufra Oasis in Libya, he left his amulets behind there. One day, in the souq in Siwa, a certain religious man approached him and said, "Give me a silver coin of twenty piasters, and we will go to your mother and ask her for a clean *gallabiya*." They did this and then walked together to a nearby spring so that my father could bathe before praying. He next took my father to the tomb of a holy man nearby and told him to put his hand inside the tomb. There the seven amulets he had lost in Libya were magically restored to him.

Today a Siwan grandmother might advise her daughter to avoid dressing her baby too well for a social gathering lest the baby attract an envious gaze. To be on the safe side, a mother will pin a silver Hand of Fatima or a *khamsa* with an Islamic inscription to her baby's clothes, and embroider a hand on the child's bonnet *(abernaas)*. When girls are dressed

46. Little *gingilt* amulets. On the right, a blue bead with seven impressions is a powerful protection.

up in their new clothes on festive occasions, many still wear a traditional string of beads comprising coral, green glass, and cowrie shells—materials that give protection against the evil eye.

In Siwa it was believed that, while the eye was deliberately used by malicious individuals, there were others who possessed the power but were unaware of this fact and so used it involuntarily. In a conversation about local beliefs, Sheib, a man in his seventies, told me,

> We knew who had the evil eye, and we would not blame them for it, but we were careful when we met them. For instance, I had an olive tree that brought three hundred *saa* a year. One day, a man I knew to have an evil eye visited me. He asked me about this tree and wanted to see it. Soon after, its branches drooped and withered and the tree died. On another occasion a precious mirror that had belonged to my father fell off the wall and smashed after a man who was known to have an evil eye visited.

In Siwa, eggs were used to remove the evil power from a victim, and even to identify the perpetrator. In the days when the belief was more prevalent, a victim would consult a particular sheikh who was highly rated as a healer. He would take an egg seven times around the patient's head while reading phrases from the Qur'an. He then broke the egg, thus symbolically annihilating the eye. Fathi Malim mentions a procedure practiced by a female magician where a special incense for the evil eye called *igawi* is burned and the name of the perpetrator revealed. As she burns the incense, she mutters a magic formula: "From the eyes of your mother, to the eyes of your father, to the eyes of the people, Evil Eye." Finally, she holds a coin over the fire, and "throws it in, signalling that the evil eye has been burned."[41]

Magic, Demons, and Healing

As well as individuals who possessed the evil eye, there were others in the community who were thought to have supernatural powers and who practiced magic, both 'black' and 'white.' Attitudes to these people were mixed. On the one hand they were respected for their special knowledge which could help solve people's problems, on the other they were feared for their sorcery which could wreck people's lives. But whether practicing magic for good or evil purposes, according to Malim, in Siwa today, "anyone associated with magic is greatly frowned upon. No one wants to marry a sorceress or into a family known to have any association with magic. Because of this fact, most magicians practice in secret, and try to publicise only their gift of healing and protecting."[42]

A magician, wise woman, fortune-teller, sorcerer, or sorceress, could be consulted in matters of love: in enabling an older girl to marry, in bringing a married couple closer, or causing a couple to divorce. They might be consulted to ensure success in business, to cast a spell against a rival, or to find something of value that has been lost. Belgrave describes how a rich merchant enlisted the aid of a wise woman to recover a large amount of his wife's silver ornaments that had been stolen. A few days later at night, on the wise woman's instructions, every member of the merchant's household, and the wise woman herself, gathered outside his house. "(T)he door was closed on the empty house." For several minutes the old woman walked up and down reciting incantations, and then "she flung open the door and led the merchant to one of the lower rooms where the missing ornaments were found lying on the floor near the window. She explained that a djinn had brought them back; the merchant paid her a reward and then she retired."[43]

Belief in the djinn—that is, in a generally ill-natured spirit that can outwit human beings—is widespread in North Africa and the Middle East. It is exemplified in traditional stories such as *A Thousand and One Nights*. Human beings have a propensity to believe in spirits and demons that are akin to the devil and for Muslims the evil djinn is such a spirit. It can appear in different forms. It can possess a person's body, a fact that is revealed by the person's strange behavior, and often by their unusual gait. It inhabits desert places, caves, pools, tombs, empty houses, and filthy places. There are also good, but capricious, djinn living in the air. Both djinn and the evil eye are mentioned in the Qur'an and accepted by Islam. In Siwa there were said to be djinn guarding the ancient tombs in the cemetery of Gebel al-Mawta, who would stop a tomb robber from taking treasure unless he first committed a particular evil act.

In Siwa, the preponderance of magical beliefs belongs to the past. The changes taking place in the town such as the street lights, the noise from construction, the new tall buildings, and the arrival of tourists have driven the djinn away. Siwans may nevertheless relate, with humor, old stories of events that befell family members or others involving the djinn. In one story, a woman was dismayed to find her husband in bed with his legs extending beyond the end of the bed when he had just left the house to go to his date garden. On a picnic in the gardens a man was amazed to see his friend kick down a bunch of dates from a tall palm tree. Another tells of what happened when a man used his wealth and power to marry a beautiful girl who was already engaged to be married. On the wedding night the girl went into a deep sleep and remained so until her husband brought a magician to see her. But the man's problems were not over. Any money he put into a security box disappeared. One night he and his wife saw a djinn in the form of a woman take the money. The djinn told him he must divorce his wife or he would go bankrupt. He decided to sell five gardens, and a house in Marsa Matrouh, and he was careful to deposit the money in the bank under a different name. As he was leaving the bank a thousand Egyptian pounds disappeared from his hand. He went to an oasis in Libya to consult a greatly respected magician, but the djinn's magic was too strong even for the magician and he died. The husband continued to suffer misfortunes, and when he slept with his wife the djinn would pull away the *tarfutet* shawl that covered them.

When a person appears to be possessed and shows physical and psychological problems, it is the local religious healer, the sheikh, who is consulted. The sheikh has the ability to exorcise evil spirits through his knowledge of the Qur'an, selecting special readings from the Holy Book. The rites will be performed over water, which the victim drinks, or over olive oil with which he or she will be anointed. He may also beat the patient's feet with palm fronds to drive out the spirits. Men come to the sheikh's house, while girls and women are generally treated at home.[44] Patients may have first tried western medicine or a traditional healer, but without any relief, before consulting the sheikh. He may find they are the victims of witchcraft, a sorcerer's curse, possession, or the evil eye. With the support of family and neighbors he will attempt to relieve the patient's condition.

There have also always been men and women in Siwa who treat physiological illnesses using medicines made from plants, animals, and minerals found in the oasis or brought from Marsa Matrouh or Alexandria.

Techniques for healing skin problems, rheumatism, and practices such as setting bones and blood letting were part of the traditional system of medicine practiced in this isolated place. The modern hospital built by the Egyptian government in 1974 to provide medical treatment is popular and well used, but many Siwans still find some traditional medicine effective, and many remain disposed to turn to homeopathic treatments and folk remedies.

8 Marriage Yesterday

The wedding was probably the most important, and was certainly the most spectacular, of the ceremonies that marked the life of a Siwan woman. It was an occasion for which the bride— in Siwi *tarust* although the Arabic word *arusa* is more commonly used now—was sumptuously bedecked with silver ornaments, the most important of which were the silver pieces her father gave her for her marriage. These would have been displayed at the bride's family home in the days before the wedding on a tray of palm fronds for relatives and neighbors to view.

The traditional marriage payment *(mahr)* comprised a fixed sum of 120 piasters—seven silver thalers—plus clothing for the bride's trousseau according to the bridegroom's means. If the bridegroom was well-to-do he would present his bride with silk robes and some silver ornaments as well. These would have been included in the financial settlement agreed before the marriage and paid to the bride's father. An exception to this might be if both families were well off. For instance, a Siwan friend told me that when he married in the 1950s, he had had no need to send any jewelry to his bride because she also came from a wealthy family, and had a lot of jewelry from her mother made by the Siwan silversmith, Gab Gab. A girl would also receive an initial gift when her suitor's mother first called at her house to convey his intentions to her mother. This was usually an item of dress or a silver thaler.

47. A Siwan girl fes-
tooned with silver
(1930s). *Marion Wasdell
and Brian de Villiers,
from: H.V. Morton,*
Through Lands of the
Bible *(London: Methuen,
1938), 208.*

If the couple divorced she would take with her the gifts that comprised the marriage payment. She would live with her parents (or an elder brother) until she remarried; and she would have to marry a man who was divorced as well. Upon remarriage, the payment she received as a divorced woman was the formal sum of 120 piasters and a token gift such as silver earrings or a pair of shoes. The wedding celebration would be a low-key family affair.

At the beginning of the twentieth century, a Siwan bride would have been about twelve to fourteen years of age and the bridegroom at least seventeen. Weddings were lengthy affairs celebrated over seven days, with elaborate ceremonies and feasting concentrated on the first three days, after which the men returned to their work in the date and olive gardens. Since the middle of the century, celebrations have become progressively less complex and now only last for two days with a women's party on the seventh day (known as the *shemata*). Reflecting the nature of Siwan society, there were separate ceremonies for men and women: some for the bride with her female family members and friends, and others for the groom and the men. Both would take place in an atmosphere of joy that included the singing of traditional songs, dancing, the reciting of prayers, the eating of special foods, and, in the case of the women, the wearing of splendid silver jewelry and silk wedding robes. During these ceremonies, the stages in the bride's transition from young girl to married woman would be distinguished by changes to her hairstyle, clothes, and jewelry. An important participant in all this was the wedding specialist, a Sudanese woman who would have arranged every detail of the wedding with the mother of the bride and who, as a foreigner, was also able to deal with male members of the family.

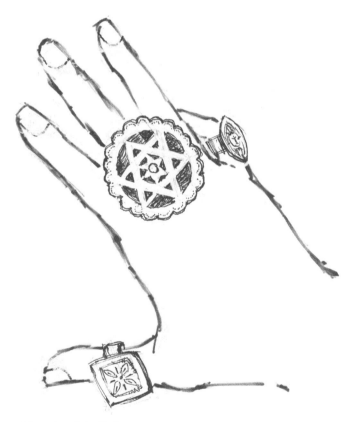

48. The large wedding ring. *John Cookson.*

Three days before the wedding, it was the custom for the bride's relatives to come and stay in order to get the house ready for the celebrations that would take place there, and to prepare the food. They came with their children on donkey carts, carrying large, round, tasseled baskets into which they had packed their festive clothes and jewelry. They also brought with them gifts they were donating to the wedding, such as ducks and pigeons and other foodstuffs.

The first act of the wedding was the signing of the local marriage contract, the *asafah*, by two male representatives from each family: it would be signed later by the bride and groom. Then, at noon at the bride's house, her female relatives and friends gathered for the ceremony called the *atras* in which the wedding specialist would create for her an intricately plaited

49. The Spring of Tamusi (1920s).
Royal Geographical Society.

new hairstyle. This style, called *tcoset*, was worn by married women. The bride sat on a decorated, palm-woven 'marriage mat' *(al-barsh)* with the incense burner for the bride *(tim shamart al-tarust)* beside her, wafting its aromatic fumes around her. The woman treated her hair with a mixture of pounded fig leaves and oil. This made it glossy and easier to plait tightly. The style demanded precision and concentration, especially the elaborate front section for which ten or twelve braids were divided at the center and wrapped smoothly across the forehead, and tied at the back. Two braids *(sawalef)* were made to hang over each cheek, and at the back at the top of her head, three braids *(le ksousa)* were made one over the other. Two plaits were made with the remaining hair. The arrangement of braids at the back of the bride's head would be completed in a ceremony after sunset.

50. The silver torque, *aghraw*, and disc, *adrim*.

It was now time for the bride's party of relations and friends to leave the house and make their way to the Spring of Tamusi for the bathing ceremony, the *atrash naman*. The bride was wearing the precious silver torque (*aghraw*) and silver disc (*adrim*) she had worn since she was ten years old. The girls first gathered up the oils and perfumes needed for the bath, and the heavy silver-chest. The wedding specialist spread the bride's green striped silk wedding gown over her shoulder and arm and the party left the house to walk through the date gardens to the spring. At the spring, a simple but important ritual was enacted in which the bride removed the silver disc from her torque. It would later be given to a younger sister to wear until her marriage, or it would be stored away with the family's wedding ornaments until it was required. The public surrendering of the *adrim*, often called the 'Virgin's Disc,' was highly symbolic. It betokened the girl's transition from childhood to mature womanhood. And it was a poignant gesture showing that she was surrendering the close protection of her own family for that of her husband's household. The girl bathed in a simple dress in the spring and the Sudanese woman washed her. She then dressed her in her silken wedding finery: the under dresses, then a red striped silk dress, and finally the mainly green, multi-colored striped silk wedding dress, the *akbir il bahrir*. She took the wedding ornaments from the jewelry box and adorned the girl with dazzling silver necklaces, headpieces, and bangles.

The wedding procession (*zaffa*) returned to the bride's house through the palm groves before sunset, the girls singing to her as they went. They were met by the bridegroom's female relatives who brought "presents of money for the bride, each according to her means" and a record was made of the contributors and the amounts they gave.[45] As the procession went on its way, rich men respectfully fastened silver coins onto the bride's shawl.[46] When it reached the town square, the bride, along with the wedding specialist, entered the tomb of Sidi Suleiman to offer prayers for a happy marriage. From this act she would also expect to gain protection from malicious glances and other evil forces, and from infertility. As she was leaving, she smudged her face with dust from the tomb.[47]

Once the bridal party had left the Spring of Tamusi, it was time for the bridegroom to take his ritual bath with his friends. Walter Cline attended this ceremony in the 1920s. He says the popular Sheikh Said was the "master of ceremonies." He washed the young man with fiber from the palm trees. The bridegroom then put on clean white pants, a traditional white robe, and a red tarboosh. The party prayed, and then left the spring for the bridegroom's house where there would be a wedding feast later in the evening with his male friends and family.[48] At the feast, the bridegroom, his eyes decorated with kohl, like many of the guests—even the old men—sat totally silent while wearing a woman's shawl over his white robe. The bride would echo this dress reversal when she was taken from her father's house to her husband's in the small hours of the next morning wrapped up in a man's *jird*, a long sheet of white wool or silk worn by Siwan and Awlad Ali Bedouin men. (In figure 3, the sheikh is wearing the *jird*.) It is an Awlad Ali custom also for the bride to be covered in this way on her journey to her husband. Exchange of garments like this during marriage festivities is practiced in different parts of North Africa. It betokens the temporary disruption of the couple's roles in society during the transformation of the bride and groom from single to married status. It is also explained as an attempt to confuse ill-intentioned spirits, and to protect the bride and groom from envious glances.

At the wedding feast, Cline "made the mistake of greeting and congratulating" the bridegroom, for "(n)o one should speak to him on this occasion, nor he to anyone; and he shyly covers his face with the woman's mantle if he wants to laugh, saying nothing. His guests all laugh and shout as merrily as they can."[49]

At the same time, there was a parallel party taking place at the bride's house. After sunset, the bridegroom's female relatives had made their way to it through the night, accompanied by a group of small boys who carried lanterns and who would play a part in the ritual, forming lines and chanting prayers. Their presence was symbolic of the girl's desire to bear male children. Mahmoud, now in his mid-fifties, told me how much he had enjoyed taking part in this ceremony when he was a child, and that the boy who read the prayers and the boy who carried the big kerosene lantern both received five piasters, while the other boys got one piaster each.

The jingle-jangle of jewelry, tinkling of bells, and swishing of silver chains announced to the guests that the bride was arriving. She took her place on the decorated marriage mat with the incense burner beside her. The wedding specialist made the finishing touches to the back of her new

51. The bride's silver and amber hair ornament, *ligsas*. *John Cookson*.

hairstyle, dividing the two plaits made earlier into five plaits each, then plaiting them together and tying them with silk thread. An important silver and amber bridal ornament called a *ligsas* was tied to the braid at the top of her head. (Two pendants ending with large pear-shaped silver plaques would be fastened to the remaining braids on the third day of the wedding and she would wear them daily after that). The final stage in the ceremony was for the wedding specialist to do the bride's henna. For the first three days the girl would sit on the marriage mat with the designs painted on her elbows resting against those on her knees, neither moving or speaking while her friends sang songs, danced, told jokes, and played games like *tora* (a game played with stones) around her. Her face and upper body would be covered with a red veil. Her stillness, her veil, and the fumes from the incense burner would protect her from malevolent forces, and separate her from normal life as she passed from being a young girl to her new married status.

When these rituals were over, the women of the bridegroom's family went home, leaving the bride, who was tired by the day's adventures, to sleep with her head in her grandmother's lap. In the middle of the night, at about 3:00 a.m., a party of the groom's family came to take her to meet her husband. Before that could happen, the dried henna had to be washed from her skin, revealing its red imprints. There then followed a series of symbolic clashes, with the groom's family trying to take her straight away, and the bride's family trying to keep her, saying that she was not quite ready, or that something was missing or needing to be straightened from her ensemble of jewelry or her dress. At last she was ready, and wrapped up in a man's *jird*. She was carried in all her heavy ornaments on the back of her father's brother (or strongest uncle), although if she or the bridegroom came from the upper class, she would be taken on the back of one of the family's servants, who was often descended from a Sudanese slave. The wedding specialist, who accompanied her, had a sword slung over her right shoulder to help ward off the evil eye.

As she was leaving her father's house for her marital home there was a lively skirmish, a mock capture of the bride by the groom's family. Then the procession made its way through the night, its path lit by flaming torches and lanterns, with the men waving their sticks and shouting to frighten away evil spirits of the night. As they reached the house, they approached it from the right, which was thought to be auspicious. The wedding specialist carried the bride across the threshold and straight up the stairs, taking care that the girl's feet never touched the ground to thwart any djinn that might follow her footsteps into the bridal room. The bridegroom had already performed rituals for the success of the marriage such as setting alight his old *gallabiya* wrapped around a palm branch on the roof. Having placed his right toe over the bride's for good luck and affirmed that she was worth her weight in silver and gold, the wedding specialist sprinkled wheat for fertility, and salt

52. A bride in all her jewelery.

against evil forces under the mattress, then left the newly married couple together. As a final precaution the bridegroom placed the sword beneath the mattress on the floor. The marriage was consummated unless the girl had not yet reached puberty. A cloth with proof of the girl's virginity was taken to the bride's mother, with a cash payment in recognition that she had raised her daughter well. The women of the bride's family rejoiced through the remainder of the night. This ritual, which was known as *abesha*, was discontinued, apparently about thirty years ago.

Because the bride was required by tradition to remain immobile during the first three days of the marriage, it was the bridegroom who removed all the pieces of her jewelry, and her clothes at night. Next morning he or a female relative would dress her and replace her jewelry, so the bridegroom's family would find her adorned as she had been the night before. He would then go to the gardens to relax with his friends.

Inevitably, details of the marriage ceremonies, the garments, and the locations where these events were held changed over time. Ahmed Fakhry says the bride was dressed in seven garments "in the evening of her marriage day,"

The first, which is next to the skin, must be white in color and of a thin transparent cloth; the second is red and transparent also; the third must be black; the fourth is yellow; the fifth is blue; the sixth is of red silk and the seventh is of green silk.[50]

In some other places in North Africa such as Sfax in Tunisia, a bride also ritually wore seven different tunics. Edward Lane, who lived in Cairo between 1825 and 1849, says rich brides in Cairo wore seven garments.[51] For every Siwan bride marrying for the first time, the important layers of her wedding costume were the green-and-striped silk wedding dress, and the red silk dress worn underneath which symbolized her fecundity. The ritual bathing used to take place at the Ayn al-Hammam spring (the Guba or Cleopatra's Spring which has been identified as the 'Spring of the Sun' mentioned by Herodotus, though there is uncertainty about the historical origins of the spring).[52] A doubtful story recounted and repeated by male travelers early in the twentieth century was that the bride's silver *adrim* was flung into the spring, to be recovered by a small boy who was a relative. Siwan women I have spoken to refute this story. They believe this important ornament was always treasured and looked after carefully, and that it would have been unthinkable to risk it by throwing it into the spring.

53. The noted 'Fountain of the Sun' (Cleopatra's Spring).

9 The Jewelry of Siwa

The most distinctive, not to say most famous, element in the costume of Siwan women was the rich collection of silver jewelry they wore on festive occasions. A married woman possessed a number of prescribed silver ornaments and beads that she wore together as a set. This comprised a round torque, silver and bead necklaces, two or three large hoop earrings worn in piercings along each ear or suspended from a red leather headband, sets of matching bangles, many rings, and hair ornaments. The pieces of jewelry she wore, and the amount of it, depended on the significance of the event and on the stage she had reached in life. At weddings she displayed copious amounts of jewelry; at family gatherings, less; and for everyday wear only a moderate set. The latter would comprise her silver torque, earrings, silver and bead necklaces, smaller rings and bangles, large tear-drop-shaped plaques suspended from her braids, and any silver or bead amulets she chose to wear in her hair or pin to her dress. As a woman grew older and was thought to be less alluring, she was less inclined to decorate herself, and required fewer amuletic pieces. She would wear only her favorite items, which always included the torque, smaller bangles, and multiple earrings. The women kept their jewelry in a wooden chest called *al-inhuli*, or a large basket *(margunah)* that was decorated with silk thread and silk tassels.

In terms of ornamentation, it was not the custom for men to wear jewelry, even rings, and a local system of time-reckoning based on the position of the sun meant that watches were hardly worn until the middle of the twentieth century. Men wore personal amulets that were leather pouches into which were stitched written papers. These amulets hung from a cord around the neck, often in multiples of three, five, or seven.

A woman received the major part of her collection of silver jewelry at the time of her marriage. This formed an asset that was entirely her property. In times of need, she could sell an item to raise funds; in times of prosperity, she could buy more pieces to add to her collection. My interviews with women in 2000 left me in no doubt that the pride they felt in wearing their jewelry was enhanced by the knowledge that it was the work of their local silversmith—a man of both technical and creative skill who is remembered as an exceptional figure in the community. This silversmith was Senoussi Daddoum Aani, known in the oasis as Gab Gab.

A woman's collection of silver ornaments combined both older and newer pieces: the jewelry she had acquired on her marriage, pieces her husband gave her later on, any she bought herself, pieces her mother-in-law lent her, and ornaments inherited from her mother or grandmother. She wore them together, and they mingled well because the forms and motifs comprised a common Siwan style that had changed but little through the years. All were decorated with a variety of symbols common to Berber peoples across North Africa: eight-pointed stars, six-pointed stars, eight-petaled rosettes, four-petaled flowers, palms, crosses, circles, almond shapes, eyebrows, zigzags, triangles, diamonds, and stylistic representations of birds, snakes, and fish. Some patterns were recognized by the women as containing elements that would provide protection or support fertility.

In Siwa, the allure of a shiny new ornament delivered straight to the customer from the silversmith's bench had special appeal. When Gab Gab's female servant brought the piece from his workshop in Manshiya, there was a flurry of excitement in the household. The woman it was made for would examine it carefully, and notice any modifications the silversmith had made to the regular patterns and motifs. It was these small changes that made the piece distinctive and personal. Examining it, she would use complimentary Siwan words like *tobahejt*, which means 'symmetrical,' 'balanced,' and 'well made,' and the word *twetwat*, which means 'shining,' and is used for silver and gold. (There is no equivalent for 'beautiful' in the Siwan language). On the other hand, *telaia* is a criticism and means 'unsymmetrical' or 'out of shape.' Even when the piece was made by one of Gab Gab's apprentices it could inspire powerful emotions in the owner. She might say, "It looks like that of the rich," and she would appreciate its shine and newness. Though 'shine' was important, and lines such as "she cleans her room 'til it shines like silver" appear in women's songs today, the women probably always preferred 'dark silver.' A young silversmith told me recently that the Siwan women who wear her jewelry say 'dark silver' is best.

The women were themselves accomplished needlewomen, basketmakers, and potters, and they expected a high level of skill and artistry from their silversmiths. The forging of metal, though, occupied a different dimension. Traditionally it had mysterious and magical connotations, and, when done well, generated awe and respect. Jewelry made by Gab Gab was highly regarded because of the level of technical skill it displayed, and for the gleam of the pure silver he used.

Gab Gab was a master of the skill of engraving, which he used extensively on flat plates. His designs on pendants and ring bezels were motifs and decorative patterns taken from the familiar world of the oasis and desert, and the sun, moon, and stars. They were engraved on plates that were basic geometric shapes: circles, squares, oblongs, ovals, and pentagons, of different sizes up to fifteen centimeters wide. Worn on festive occasions with long silver chains and pierced pendants and beads, the simple forms and clearly delineated engraved designs visibly enhanced the ensemble.

The bright color of silver was important to the Berber peoples. The Siwans compare silver to water for its clarity, purity, and curative properties. In fact, they have sayings such as "the silver is as clear as water" or "the silver is as pure as water." Women say that silver was beneficial in many ways and could help solve their problems: worn against the skin it would heal a wound or alleviate the pain of the sting of a scorpion. It might give a shock and thus improve a medical condition: silver is an excellent conductor of electricity. A magician in the oasis told me that he had advised parents who required amulets for their children about the many benefits of wearing silver, for instance in helping a child sleep through the night.

Hollow silver spherical beads, or large silver rhomboid-shaped beads, were included in most of the silver necklaces or headpieces women wore. They threaded their own beads following a set mathematical formula for each type. They used a traditional palette of amber, red coral, black, and green glass. They were rarely tempted to incorporate a new item from the variety of beads and trinkets that peddlers and other travelers brought in their baggage as trading items. Some of their beads were genuine stones and substances: coral from the Mediterranean; amber from the Baltic (or copal resin or amboid, pressed amber); and onyx from India. Others were cheaper synthetic plastic or glass imitations. Indeed, Siwan necklaces donated by a traveler to the British Museum in 1920 show that glass imitations of coral were sometimes intermixed with the genuine article. Even two hundred years ago, Horneman noted in his description of the jewelry worn by Siwan women that "their necklace is glass imitating coral."[53]

Glass beads had been traded in North Africa since ancient times, from Pharaonic Egypt, Carthage, Hellenistic Alexandria, Islamic Cairo, and from India. From the end of the fifteenth century, glass beads began to be exported to Africa in great quantities from Europe. And the glassmakers of Bohemia were soon making beads and bead materials specifically for Islamic countries.

54. Small *gingilt* amulets.
John Cookson.

Many of the stone and glass beads the Siwans wore had particular homeopathic or prophylactic qualities, and an ensemble of jewelry would therefore include items that were chosen to meet the wearer's personal prescription. The Berbers believed that amber had medicinal and healing qualities, and that red coral supported fertility and would ward off the evil eye. Siwan women incorporated small heart-shaped or oval amulets called *gingilt* that comprised a colored stone or glass piece framed in silver into certain necklaces. These *gingilt* could be bought from a shop in the town. A *gingilt* with a sky blue stone was popular, and a green one—green like the vegetation—was particularly highly prized. It was worn to boost fertility, or a woman would pin it over her heart if she and her husband were unhappy together and he would come to her. A green gingilt could also relieve stresses, worries, and a headache. A dark red stone signified blood and fertility. Stones could also be worn out of sight next to the skin to perform an intimate and private rather than a social purpose. A white stone bead was threaded on cotton and pinned next to the breast to ensure a good supply of milk for a baby.

A seventy-eight-year-old-woman called Guia showed me the tin of stones and silver *khamsa*s she had saved as keepsakes. Among them there was a roughly polished and perforated brown stone, "a good stone," she says, that is prized for its magical powers. In her collection she also had a gold stone, a half-black-half-white stone that a female relative brought from Mecca, and a ring set with white agate embellished with a large black dot that her teenage granddaughter Marwa sometimes wears.

Festival and Ceremony

A woman decked herself out in her festive silver on occasions such as *eids* and weddings, when she helped her relatives deliver the bride's trousseau to her marital home on the second day of the wedding, to celebrate the return of a pilgrim from Mecca, and when she went to welcome a newborn on the third day after the birth, and again on the seventh day for the birth ceremony.

When making ready to attend such occasions, an important task was to assemble and prepare the ornaments she would wear. Some had to be cleaned with sand and lemon, or with salty water. Sometimes, the shopping lists women gave to male relatives when they made their excursions to Alexandria would include a special powder for polishing silver called *dakik* which could be bought from the *attar* in the Souq al-Attarine who sold medicinal herbs, incense, and henna. Sorting out the jumble of ornaments in her silver chest or jewelry basket, she also set aside any pieces that had gotten broken and should be taken to Gab Gab to be repaired.

When Siwan women gathered for a celebration, they would be bedecked in a dazzling display of cascading silver chains and dangles. Those of limited means would have few pieces of their own but would have been lent pieces by richer relations and neighbors. Women say they all felt enormous pride in wearing the jewelry. An elderly woman, Aisha, told me, "Everybody felt so special, whether the rich wearing a lot of big pieces in the purest silver, or the poor in smaller pieces made in cheaper metal." Another woman said, "Wearing it put me in high spirits! Yes, my jewelry was heavy but I didn't notice its weight. I liked the feeling of the leather tight around my head." She was referring to the red leather headband construction from which her heavy hoop earrings (*is-sudan*) were suspended. The jewelry also performed a role in drawing together the Westerners and Easterners. All wore the same collection of ornaments.

55. A jewelry basket. *Musée d'ethnographie, Geneva.*

"There was no difference," Aisha said, "unless we were looking for it!" The brilliance, size, and quantity of the pieces were a visible demonstration of the power and confidence of the group.

Ornaments Used as Ritual Objects

As well as forming part of the mass of ornaments women wore to festive occasions, individual pieces were used as ritual objects to ensure health and protection in the special ceremonies that marked the transitional stages in a person's life, such as the birth ceremony, the circumcision of a boy, and the pilgrimage to Mecca.

The Birth Ceremony: Smashing the Bowl

On the seventh day after a birth it was the custom for women to perform a ritual designed to transmit good wishes for the child's wellbeing. Belgrave says they first removed their silver bangles and placed them in a clay bowl filled with water. They raised the bowl seven times, and then let it crash to the ground.[54] The act of smashing the bowl, and the resound-

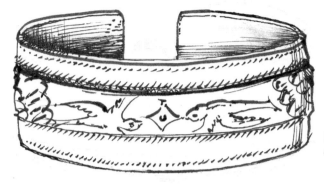

56. The silver bangle, *dimjun. John Cookson.*

57. The silver bangle, *suar. John Cookson.*

ing noise it made, was believed to drive away malicious forces, and especially the dangerous djinn that play with children. Touching the bowl may also have been a charm relating to fertility.

In place of a bangle, another ring-shaped piece worn by the mother might be used instead. Walter Cline, in the 1920s, said, "The midwife unties from the mother's hair an ornamental silver or lead ring, and sinks it in an *ajrang* of water. . . . Holding one of her own fingers in this water, [the midwife] blesses the other women in extravagant terms, and daubs

58. A ceremonial pot, *ajr*

each woman's face with henna."[55] The bowl was then carried to the top of the house and dropped from the roof.

When I went to stay in Siwa in 1999, this ritual was still being performed. A silver piece, and henna, salt, and coins such as one-piaster pieces, were placed in a metal bowl of water. The henna turned the water red and was a symbol of fertility; the silver bangle promised the child good health and protection; salt was cleansing and protective; and the coins would bring good fortune. When the bowl crashed to the ground with a loud clatter, the children of the neighborhood ran to gather up the coins.

The Circumcision Rite

A silver bangle was used in a circumcision rite performed by a boy's mother the night before his operation, when she ceremonially placed her bangle in a clay pot of water.[56] The rite demonstrated the link between mother and son, and, poignantly, the detachment from her as he symbolically entered adulthood. Her good wishes for him were expressed through the beneficial and healthful properties of silver and water, which would assist the healing of the boy's wounds. The form of the ceremonial pot or *ajrang*, a domestic vessel which has a spout for pouring, may have significance for the Siwans. In Egypt, pots with gender-specific forms—a spout (*ibria*) for a boy and a wide mouth (*qulleh*) for a girl—are purchased for the birth ceremony.

Rolling the Silver Bangles: A Farewell to the Pilgrims

The most spectacular use of a piece of silver jewelry for ritual purposes took place in a ceremony that marked the departure of Siwan pilgrims for Mecca. In the days before the tarmac road from Marsa Matrouh was built, Siwa was only linked to the outside world by lengthy camel routes that were uncomfortable and dangerous. A ceremony was therefore held to bestow good fortune on the departing pilgrims, in which the women's heavy silver bangle, the *suar*, was the centerpiece. The whole community, dressed in white, gathered by a spring at the eastern boundary of the oasis. In the 1920s, Belgrave attended this important ceremony. He described what happened next:

> A near relative takes from the wife of the pilgrim her round silver bangles and rolls them along the ground, a distance of about a hundred yards, to where the husband stands facing the east. The wife . . . dressed entirely in white, runs along behind him and gathers up a little sand from each place where the bracelets stopped rolling and fell to the ground. She puts the sand carefully into a little leather bag.[57]

59. Palm fronds showing an occupant has gone to Mecca on the Hajj.

The powers that women assigned to the silver bangles, and the dramatic effects they made as they skimmed across the sand ablaze with the light of the sun, surely betokened the safe-keeping of the pilgrims on their journey across the desert. A woman gave me her interpretation of the ritual: "The bangle made a ring around our sins. The grains of sand were our sins." The pilgrims said their farewells and the caravan went on its way. The people returned home singing to the beat of drums. When the pilgrim's family reached home they went up on the roof and fixed three palm fronds that had been cut down at the spring to one corner, and tied the little bag of sand to the tips of the fronds so they bent eastward toward Mecca. Two months later, when it was thought the pilgrims would have reached their destination, the bag of sand was pierced. Letting the sand run away symbolized the cleansing of the pilgrim's sins. The dried palm branches were only taken down from the roof when at last news reached the town that the pilgrims' caravan was approaching the oasis on its return. Sheep were sacrificed and feasts prepared, to be held in their honor.

Widowhood

In the past, when a man died, his wife would take off every piece of her jewelry. She was expected to stay in seclusion for four months and ten days. She was labeled the *gulah*—the female ghost—because she was in a separate realm, apart from society. She was regarded as being socially polluting and it was believed she might bring bad luck to anyone she looked at. This ritual may have related to the difficult life the woman faced as widow.

Certain restrictions were imposed, such as prohibiting her from wearing her jewelry, changing her dress, decorating her eyes with kohl or her skin with henna, cutting her nails, or doing her hair. These limitations lasted for four months and ten days and showed respect for her husband and her family and might also prevent any disaster befalling them or the community.[58]

The beginning and conclusion of the Siwan widow's period of seclusion was marked by a ritual bath at the Spring of Tamusi. Abdallah, writing in 1917, says that "when the funeral of her husband moves toward the grave," the widow, in the company of her friends, takes her bath. "She cuts off the two thick braids of hair which have hung over her shoulders, musses her careful row of bangs, cuts her toe nails and finger nails and dons a white or green dress."[59] At the end of the long period of isolation, the mourning restrictions were lifted and the widow's female relatives assisted her in bathing at sunrise at the Spring of Tamusi or her nearest spring. The woman was ritually cleansed of her link with death and the supernatural and her imagined power to cast the evil eye. She put on clean clothes, and her beads and silver necklaces and bangles. Her hair was oiled and braided and silver pieces tied once more to her tresses. Freed from her polluted state, she was ritually reincorporated into the community with a new status and role. From then on she was able to remarry.

10 Silver Ornaments and Colored Beads

The mass of silver jewelry and beads in a Siwan woman's jewelry box
was transformed into a well-ordered, decorative arrangement when
she put them on. Each piece had its place in the symmetrical design
that covered her upper body. These were standard pieces worn by
everybody, but the rich were able to afford quantities of high-grade silver
ornaments and precious beads. The amount of jewelry a woman carried on
special occasions could weigh up to five kilos.

The Silver Necklaces
Adrim and Aghraw

The most important and beautiful pieces of Siwan jewelry are the round,
silver torque called *aghraw*, and the large, shield-like, engraved silver disc,
the *adrim*, that was suspended from it by a silver loop. The torque closure
is a hook and eye; the eye being formed by folding back and wrapping the
wire six or seven turns on both sides. These pieces were worn by Siwans
for hundreds of years and their continued existence was noted at the end
of the eighteenth century by Horneman.[60] They presumably owe a debt to
the Germanic Vandals, a semi-nomadic tribe who settled in North Africa
in the fifth century, and the Byzantines who conquered them over a
hundred years later in 533 and 544. The Germanic tribes are famous for
their splendid jewelry. Circular disc ornaments such as pendants with a

suspension loop were typical and might be inspired by Roman coins. Granulation and filigree were techniques used for enrichment.[61] Large gold discs were worn by wealthy women in Cairo into the nineteenth century.

The Siwan silversmith Gab Gab made the *adrim* pendant in different weights and dimensions so that girls of different heights could wear it comfortably. The disc of a small girl, for example, might be twelve centimeters in diameter, while that of a bigger girl could reach fifteen centimeters. Her torque and disc together could weigh as much as a kilo. Girls began to wear the *adrim* on social occasions from about the age of ten to indicate their marriageability. It appears there was no special ceremony to mark this change of status. In wealthy families, each daughter of marriageable age would have her own *adrim*, but poorer families might have only one that was handed down from the eldest to the younger daughters. The silver disc played an important role for a girl, and symbolically discarding it formed the focus of a ritual performed on the day of her marriage at the Spring of Tamusi. In fact, it was worn again with her wedding ornaments, though placed behind the precious silver cylinder and chains of an amuletic piece called a *tashabat*.

Old surviving *adrim* are all decorated with an equilateral cross, an ancient and widespread symbol of the cosmos. The bands of the cross and the border are ornamented with engraved and punched patterns of dots, hatching, cross-hatching, and scallops that produced glistening effects in sunlight or lamplight. The center of the cross is emphasized by a round boss or bulla. The bulla of some of the older *adrim* are surrounded by small balls of silver (granulation) and the bulla is engraved with a tiny eight-pointed star. Each of the four spaces between the arms of the cross is filled with a matching eight-pointed star, rayed star, shooting star, or rosette. The wide silver loop through which the torque is threaded is engraved with a geometric diamond pattern. Geometric figures such as the cross and the eight-pointed star that decorate the disc recall designs that were used in the ancient Mediterranean.

Siwan women wore the torque daily at home,

60. A girl wearing the *adrim* and *aghraw*.

and on special occasions with their festive jewelry. A woman of seventy, called Mabrouka, told me that it was worn as a protection "against the bad people" and as a decoration, "to make us attractive to our husbands." The torque was greatly valued by the women, and Mabrouka, who had inherited a lot of Gab Gab's jewelry from her mother, said she had worn the *aghraw* he made until the end of the 1980s when she could no longer resist offers from traders to buy it from her. Selling it had made her very unhappy but she had needed to buy medicines. "I cried for three days when I sold it," she said.

The *adrim* is a famous piece and its influence can be seen in silver discs that have been found far from Siwa. For instance, an early twentieth-century Moroccan necklace with seven discs resembling the Siwan *adrim* comes from the valley of Ziz near a caravan route that ran across North Africa through Siwa.[62] Today, in the silver souq in Cairo and even in glass cases of department stores in Paris and London, replicas of the Siwan disc and torque, or new interpretations of the disc, can be found.

Tashabat

Another fine piece is the *tashabat*: a large, silver, tubular amulet case, approximately fifteen centimeters in length, which was worn by wealthy brides. Silver chains are suspended from each of the seven rings along the base, and from a ring at each end. The chains terminate with large spherical bells. Early pieces, made by Master Gab Gab in high-content silver, are finely engraved with floral and arabesque designs. Later versions, decorated with embossed foliate designs, were made for the Siwans by the silversmith Amin of Alexandria, in lower-grade silver or base metal. Cases such as these, which are worn throughout the Middle East, are designed to hold verses from the Qur'an or magic invocations written on pieces of paper. Even if they are empty, they are believed to possess the power to divert evil from the wearer.

Only the rich ordered the silver *tashabat* from Gab Gab. For others there was a colorful amulet that a woman could make in her home. It was an oblong, flat pad, covered in red goat's skin, and ornamented with silk embroidery, small silver coins, and mother-of-pearl buttons. Chains that ended with large bells were suspended from the bottom, and there were leather loops along the top. A bride wore the silver or leather amulet in front of the *adrim*, suspended from the torque.

All the leather accessories for jewelry were cut out by the women from skins they say came from Cairo.

61 and 62. (Left) A silver *tashabat* amulet; and (right) a decorated leather substitute for the silver tashabat. *Musée d'ethnographie, Geneva.*

Silver and Bead Necklaces
Salhayat

The *salhayat* consists of six matching, openwork crescent-shaped pendants, strung with red coral and silver beads. The corals are composites of three cylinders or threaded in bundles of three. A bride wore this necklace with all her wedding jewelry.

The deep crescent, *hilal*, encloses a variety of designs. There is usually a five- or six-pointed star (or flower, rosette, or sun wheel equivalent) surrounded by floral and foliate patterns, and snake, bird, and fish motifs. Another quite different design represents a face or mask dominated by large eyes, presumably to confront the evil eye. It has been compared to the Gorgo-Medusa amulets of the Roman period.[63] A short central prong is a feature of the pendants, and may represent a snake's head, phallus, or the root of a tree.

The Siwan women wore *hilal*s made by their local silversmiths or imported into Siwa along the trade routes from the west, especially from Tunisia. They also acquired *hilal*s from Awlad Ali Bedouin in exchange for dates.[64] The pendants were made in different grades of silver and in various sizes, the largest being about ten centimeters in length. Wearing pieces of this size would demonstrate the affluence of the family.

After the wedding, a bride continued to wear the *salhayat* necklace every day for its obvious decorative value, to support her desire for children, and for its powers of protection because she was still believed to be vulnerable

63. *Salhayat* necklaces. *John Cookson.*

to envy. A surprising feature of these necklaces is that the end of a prong of a pendant is sometimes missing. It has been said that this is because they were broken off on purpose after the birth of a son.[65] However, on several occasions elderly Siwan women told me that these pendants were too valuable ever to have been treated in this way. It may be that they were occasionally clipped off to solve a temporary need for money by a traveler or a Siwan.

Timisnakt

The *timisnakt* consists of a short bead necklet of silver spherical beads, red coral cylinders, and green glass beads, from which hang up to twelve long chains ending with five-sided (pentagonal) plates. The matching, engraved plates hang below the waist. Sometimes, set into the chains at intervals, there are small colored beads and amuletic green glass beads inscribed with the Islamic crescent and star and framed in silver. The *timisnakt* necklace was worn only by girls before marriage. The rattle of the metal plates in movement would chase away mischievous spirits. Movement and sound were important considerations in the design of certain ornaments,

64. A *timisnakt* necklace.
Musée d'ethnographie, Geneva.

and women referred to the pieces that made sounds such as the large jingling bells and thick rustling chains as *tchunchinchun*—noisy. However, tinkling ornaments such as hollow bangles and anklets that contained pebbles or bits of metal that were worn across the Middle East were not a feature of Siwan jewelry.

The pentagonal plates come in different sizes, from four to seven centimeters in length. An engraved border defines the shape, and frames the field that displays a motif derived from the natural world such as a stylistic representation of a palm branch, or a palm tree with a bunch of dates hanging on each side. The field may be divided into compartments (a characteristic also of Libyan and Tunisian jewelry) each containing a fish, a flower, foliage, and so on.

There is sometimes a larger pentagonal plate, or a triangular openwork pendant called *tilaksit*, in the center of the necklace.[66] A typical *timisnakt* necklace that was donated to the British Museum in 1920 has seven plaques including a *tilaksit* pendant in the center. Another, given at the same time, has a different assemblage[67]: the plaques are threaded directly onto the necklet and from them are suspended chains from which hang small silver hands—the fingers represented by a saw-edge—and small plates that take the basic form of the *salhayat* pendant, some cut from coins. The sharp points emphasize the prophylactic function of the necklace.

65. Plates of the *timisnakt* necklace. *John Cookson.*

Tilaksit

This is a triangular cast openwork pendant. As well as being attached to jewelry, it is worn on clothes. *Tilaksit* is the Siwan word for the shape and size of the piece of bread used to scoop food from a tray and placed in the mouth when eating. The *tilaksit* pendant is similar to the small triangular fibulae worn by Berber women in the Aurés of Algeria, made using the openwork technique. Intriguingly, it also resembles triangular cast silver or gold plaques that were made in China between the eleventh and fourteenth centuries. These incorporate floral and animal designs and were probably made to stitch to garments. They were ideal small and precious items merchants could carry in their baggage along the Silk Road.

66. *Tilaksit* pendants.

Bead Necklaces

All bead necklaces are threaded with cotton. For the fastener, a loop is made from the remaining thread at one end, and a bead at the other end fits through the loop. A blue, green, or bright yellow bead is placed next to the fastener (and I have also seen a black and white banded 'eye bead' and small gold beads used)[68] to protect the wearer and the precious necklace itself from an envious look.

Suweidi

The *suweidi* is a short necklace of coral, onyx, and silver beads that exhibits striking red and black stripes. The intricate threading begins with a silver bead followed by multi-stranded threading of tiny round onyx beads and coral cylinders using a bead-netting technique.[69] The net of beads falls into precisely aligned stripes when it is hung around the neck. This is an unusual necklace for Siwa, although netting techniques are widely used in Bedouin beadwork, by African peoples to the south, and in the oasis of Bahariya in a colorful necklace made with tiny beads.

The *suweidi* necklace was included in a bride's ensemble of jewelry, and she continued to wear it after her marriage. The symbolism of the color red was important because her fertility would be enhanced and she would gain protection from the evil eye. The *suweidi* is still a favorite, though married women, who these days wear gold jewelry, prefer to leave out the silver beads when threading their necklaces. At weddings some unmarried girls like to wear the *suweidi*. Adorning a child in this way may still show a grandmother's concern to protect her when she is dressed-up and at her most vivacious at social events.

67. A *suweidi* necklace.

Aras Negbesen

The *aras negbesen* comprises a longer string of cowrie shells, coral cylinder beads, and green glass beads. Precious, amuletic, flat green glass beads inscribed with the star and crescent motif may be incorporated into the necklace. An alternative *aras negbesen* necklace is made entirely of cowrie shells. The *aras negbesen* was worn by a bride during ceremonies and after the wedding to boost her fertility and protect her from the evil eye. Some brides today still wear these beads after the wedding, and young girls wear them for the *eid*s when they go out in their best clothes to meet their friends.

Ilazim

Worn by young unmarried girls and young married women, this necklace is not worn in Siwa now, but was important in the past. The *ilazim* was expensive, being made up of large amber beads and silver beads, often with the addition of coral.

The *ilazim* necklaces I have seen in the oasis are threaded in sequence with three silver beads followed by an amber bead, then by a bunch of three cylindrical coral beads (or a similar composite bead), then by an amber bead, and the pattern is repeated. Glass or synthetic plastic imitations often replaced the coral and amber in these necklaces. As a result they lost their former aesthetic and monetary value, but remained a colorful and talismanic adornment.

68. An *ilazim necklace. Musée d'ethnographie, Geneva.*

Head and Hair Ornaments
Lugyeet

The *lugyeet* or *e-sudan* consists of a red leather headband construction, decorated with mother-of-pearl buttons, from which hang three flat metal hoops of Libyan origin, or similar silver hoops made by Gab Gab, over each ear. The heavy Libyan earrings are stamped with simple flower, birds-in-flight, or sun motifs along the base of the hoop. They have a hook and eye fastening similar to that of the torque. This form of earring *(sad)* was also worn in Tunisia. Gab Gab's silver earrings, which were lighter than the imported Libyan ones, could be worn through two or three piercings in the ear. Girls wore multiple earrings, similar to their mothers. It was the custom for women and girls to suspend large mother-of-pearl buttons or perforated silver piasters from the rings. Some boys, irrespective of social status, also wore an earring in one ear until the age of three or four.

69. Lugyeet. Musée d'ethnographie, Geneva.

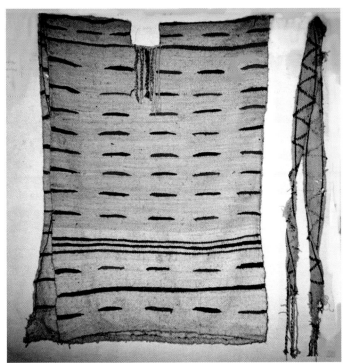

Laborer's tunic, *jubit*, worn by *zaggala*.

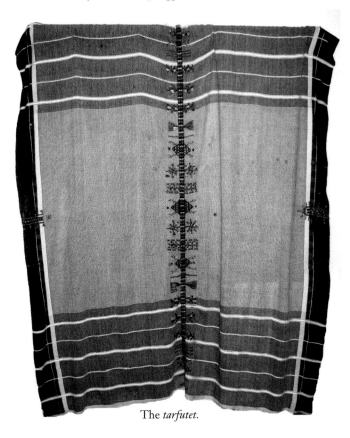

The *tarfutet*.

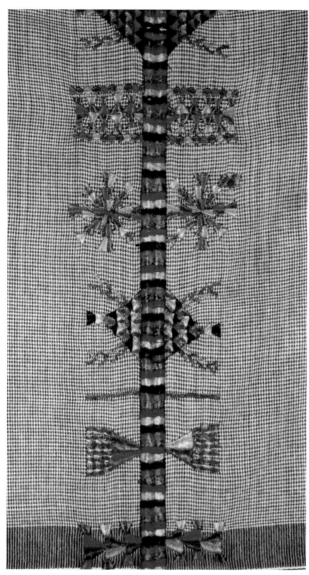

Detail of the embroidery across the center of the *tarfutet*.

Detail of embroidery with 'hands' worn at the forehead.

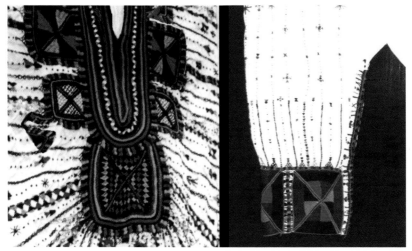

The seal, *khatem*, motif is composed of triangles and decorates
the neckline of the wedding dress and the cuffs of the trousers.

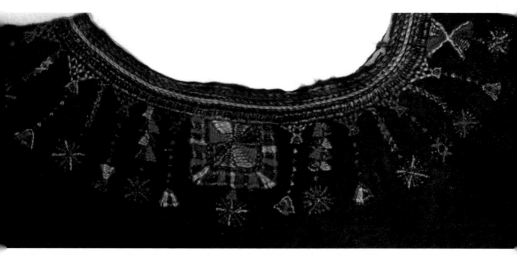

The seal, *khatem*, motif is often embroidered at the back neckline of a wedding tunic.

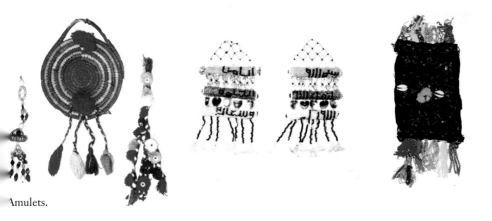

Amulets.

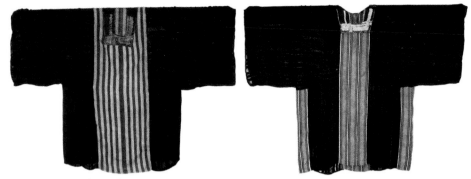

Women's traditional tunics.

A woman's satin-striped green tunic. *Musee d'ethnographie, Geneva.*

An embroidered square collar, incorporating a protective coiled pattern, worn by married women.

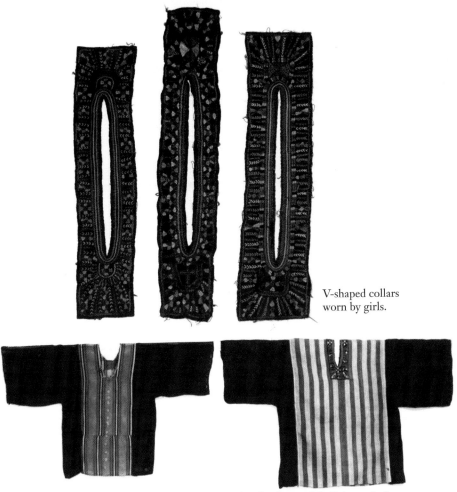

V-shaped collars
worn by girls.

Children's tunics: (right) with a traditional embroidered collar; and (left) instead of
the collar, a mother has stitched a pattern around the neckline and embroidered buttons emulating an urban style.

(Right) A machine-embroidered *akbir nwasa* dress; (center) a *natiyac* gallabiya;
and (left) a yellow satin-striped polyester *akbir nwasa* dress.

Red goatskin shoes, *zrabin.*
Musée d'ethnographie, Geneva.

A decorated leather *kohl* pot for the bride,
tangkult. Musée d'ethnographie, Geneva.

Detail of a wedding tunic embroidered with motifs: 'bride,' 'lantern,' 'fish,'
'sun,' and 'hand'—depicted with three fingers which is acceptable.

Detail of the frontal panel of a wedding tunic embellished with mother-of-pearl buttons.

The red silk dress was an important layer of the bride's costume.

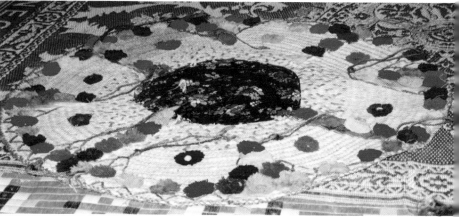

The marriage mat, *al-barsh*.

Detail from a modern *troket*. The sequinned patterns obscure the tiny traditional embroidered motifs.

The 'new embroidery,' decorating a hem patch *litshineb nagil ilharir*, incorporates some traditional motifs: 'water-jug,' 'bride,' and 'bucket.'

Detail of a *troket* with sun motifs stitched with different colored threads—depicting 'fives'.

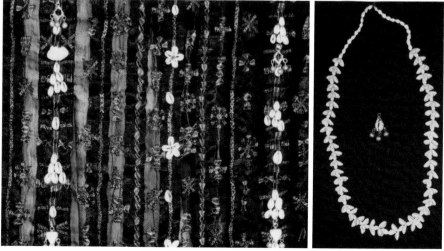

Cowries decorating a *troket* head shawl, an amulet, and an *aras negbesen* necklace.

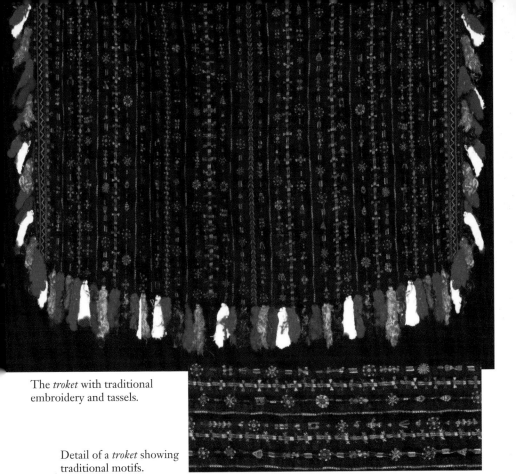

The *troket* with traditional
embroidery and tassels.

Detail of a *troket* showing
traditional motifs.

Detail of a striped *troket nakbir ilharir* with traditional embroidery. The modern
sequin embellishment depicts 'palm branch,' 'bird,' and 'bride' motifs.

Detail of a *troket* showimg stitches.

An embroidered black wedding tunic, *asherah hawak azdhaf*.

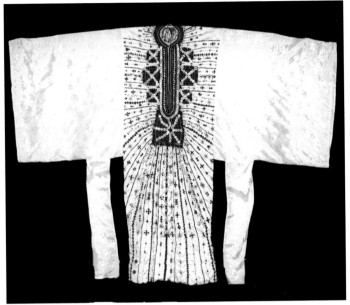

An embroidered
white wedding
tunic, *asherah nauak.*

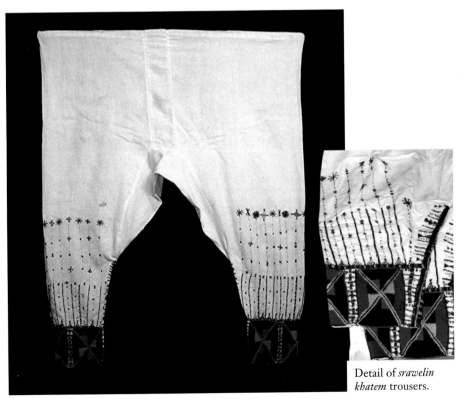

Detail of *srawelin
khatem* trousers.

Embroidered trousers, *srawelin khatem.*

A wedding tunic with *gutan* ropes.

Detail of a frontal panel decorated with auspicious mother-of-pearl buttons.

Opposite: The front of a wedding tunic.

A wedding dress from the Oasis of Dakhla in the Western Desert.

A textile made in the 1980s.

70. Earrings threaded with a coin and mother-of-pearl buttons.

Tilakeen

A particularly beautiful crescent head decoration, the *tilakeen*, was worn by a bride. These large silver crescents that were worn suspended over her ears were delicately engraved by Gab Gab with floral or arabesque designs. From them were suspended long silver chains ending with large bells. Old photos show Siwan girls wearing the *tilakeen* suspended from their braids, from a chain worn over the head, or from a red leather headband construction. Headpieces such as these, with long chains hanging from them, derive from Roman and Byzantine jewelry.

71. *Tilakeen. Musée d'ethnographie, Geneva.*

Gertrude Simpson, a visitor to Siwa in the 1920s, mentioned a piece that was suspended inside the crescent (which I have only seen in an old photo). She described it picturesquely as

> a very curious ornament . . . . worn by unmarried girls. It is composed of mother-of-pearl three or four inches in length and an inch broad . . . . and hangs down over the cheek. A round piece of two inches in diameter is attached to this. On the nuptial night it is taken away under protest, and can never be worn again.[70]

Ligsas

The *ligsas* was an important hair pendant worn by the bride at the back of her head. The threading of the piece comprises a large silver rhomboid-shaped bead followed by a large amber bead (often a cube), then a large silver ring from which are suspended two or three silver *khamesa* amulets such as a cylindrical amulet case, hand of Fatima, or fish, all with five bells along the bottom.

72. *Ligsas* and *ligsussia* with *taziri* (moon) plaques. *John Cookson.*

A different *ligsas* ornament ends with a large pear-shaped silver plaque called *taziri*, moon. The elegant design that Master Gab Gab engraved on the plaque seems to represent a starry, moonlit sky. Two were added to the bride's plaits during the wedding festivities. I have heard a story that placing one of the *tizareteen* to the front would disclose to a woman's mother-in-law she was having trouble with her husband!

A third type of *ligsas* hair pendant ends instead with a triangular-shaped piece, *tilaksit*, from which are suspended chains ending with bells. This piece was draped across the forehead, and hung in an alluring fashion over the temple.

Tadlilt

The *tadlilt* is an unusual red leather bridal head-dress. It comprises a headband from which hang up to twelve leather straps, reaching to just above the shoulders. They are decorated with amber beads, though I have seen later versions that are studded with mother-of-pearl buttons or sparkling colored glass and plastic buttons. The straps end with silver rings and bells. In this headdress the Siwan bride would have resembled women depicted in Ancient Egyptian wall paintings wearing diadems and decorated braids or wigs.

Small Pieces For the Hair

At the center front of her braided hairdo, a woman would wear a silver *khamsa* such as a triangular or rectangular flat plate inscribed with religious verses, a small cylindrical amulet case, or a Hand of Fatima—all with five bells dangling from them. Gab Gab made these pieces in high-grade silver for his Siwan customers. Inexpensive cast crescent and tear-shaped plates in low-content silver bearing Qur'anic inscriptions, which were made in Cairo and worn widely in Egypt, were included among these ornaments that could be worn in the hair. Amulets such as these were used across the Middle East against the evil eye and the djinn.

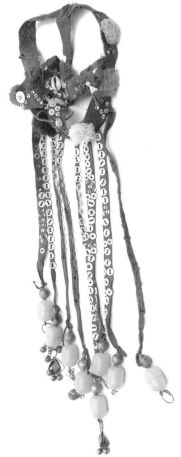

73. *Tadlilt. Musée d'ethnographie, Geneva.*

The women wove a few amuletic pieces, such as silver piaster coins and engraved silver discs made by their local silversmiths, into their braids. Siwans used only the smaller silver coins as amulets to decorate their hair or link through their earrings. Some other Egyptian groups and Berber peoples west of Siwa used the large Spanish/Mexican pillar-dollar and Maria Theresa thaler to decorate their necklaces or veils.

Bangles

Siwan women had open bangles. Married women wore a matching bangle *dimjun* on each wrist daily. This bangle is decorated with birds in flight and fishes on either side of an eye-shaped motif. It was the narrowest of the bangles but was still heavy and valuable. This bangle remains a favorite of many elderly Siwans, who continue to wear it in the traditional fashion.

A pair of massive cuff-like bangles *(suar)* was worn by a bride and, after her wedding, on festive occasions. Even when gold was becoming fashionable in the oasis, women continued to wear them with the embroidered wedding costume, with red henna patterns adorning their hands. The bangle is decorated at the front and back with a large floral motif that may represent a sunflower, and the center of the flower is marked by a large boss. At each side of the bangle there is a thick rivet, fixed with three bosses.

This piece was made by Cairene silversmiths for the women of the oases of the Western Desert and the Awlad Ali Bedouin. Siwan Hajj Mustapha, who at the age of seventeen did some training in the local silversmiths' workshop with Master Gab Gab's successor Muhammad Abugsessa, told me that Gab Gab also made these bangles. The design is distinctly Libyan and Berber. Wide bangles of similar form are found across North Africa; silversmiths in Algeria often used large cabochon corals in place of the silver bosses.

An alternative, wide (though much lighter) bangle, the *diblitsh*, which was worn in Siwa, is decorated with a linear palm branch (or eyebrow) pattern either side of a central longitudinal ridge. Two small flowers are stamped each side of the opening. This bangle was made in Cairo for women of the Western Desert.

Rings

The silver rings, in the form of signet rings, are regarded as being among the most beautiful pieces of Siwan jewelry. Each ring *(mahbis)* comprises a flat, engraved bezel attached to a simple shank. The rings were worn in

74. A selection of Gab Gab's silver rings including a Star of David wedding ring.
John Cookson.

multiples, on every finger *(tad)* except the index finger, which points upward in prayer. The three remaining fingers and the thumb were each assigned their own shape and size of ring: for the thumb *(tad azar)* the ring was square, for the ring finger *(tad namas)* it was oblong, for the little finger *(tad akeeka)* there was a smaller leaf-shaped ring. The middle finger *(tad namas)* took a large round ring worn by a bride. The bride's ring was on average 6 centimeters in diameter, and extended over three fingers.

There was an endless variety of geometric and floral motifs to choose from in Gab Gab's pages of jewelry designs, depicting the sun, the eight-pointed star, and the foliage and fruit of the date palm and olive tree. One abstract pattern sketched, with a few straight lines, the abundance of foliage and mesh and interlacing of palm branches. An unusual wedding ring was a large, openwork six-pointed star formed by the intersection of two equilateral triangles. This design, sometimes called a Star of David, is used on silver jewelry throughout the Maghreb.[71]

Motifs that decorate the rings are often engraved within compartments. Frequently, the central motif of the bezel plate of a ring is depicted within a diamond or circle, and resembles an eye. Worn on public occasions on most fingers of the hands, the 'eyes' would mesmerize the envious gaze.

Anklets

Little boys and girls wore silver anklets decorated with tinkling bells. Women say the bells entertained the child, encouraged an infant to walk, and helped the mother locate the child when out of sight. The noise would also frighten away mischievous spirits. Old people in Siwa have no recollection of women wearing anklets, but they may once have worn them. Horneman, who was in Siwa for only a week at the end of the eighteenth century, said that the Siwan women decorated their "arms and legs (just above the ankle), with rings of silver, of copper, or of glass."[72] Siwan women did not wear a nose ring although women of the other oases of the Western Desert wore anklets and a nose ring. For example, in Bahariya, married women had plain silver anklets, and a nose ring made of gold (to avoid infection) that was worn in the right side of the nose. Ahmed Fakhry says in his book *Bahariyah and Farafra* (first published in 1974), that until the 1950s there were two smiths making silver jewelry for the women in al-Bawiti, the capital of Bahariya, who were Copts. After that time, women then acquired jewelry made for them in Cairo or al-Fayoum.[73]

Silver Marks

When the personal relationship between silversmith and customer in the towns gave way to mass production and selling from shops, it became necessary for the government to guarantee the silver content by hallmarking items. The marks are framed in squares, the first showing a lotus flower (or before 1946, a cat); the second, the percentage of silver (sixty, eighty, or ninety percent) in Arabic numerals with the particular assay office denoted above; and the third giving the date.

Hallmarking became increasingly common in Egypt after its introduction in 1916, but it was not common or required in rural areas where a smith worked for the domestic market. Siwa's remote location and the fact that Gab Gab was well known in the community and used silver supplied by the customer made it unnecessary. However, some of the pieces that were made in Cairo for the peoples of the Western Desert do bear hallmarks. The wide *diblitsh* and *suar* bangles Muhammad Mikawi made, for example, are stamped with a hallmark and his name. Mikawi, who was an important silversmith and merchant with a silver shop and workshop in the Khan al-Khalili souq, was well-known for creating these bangles, as was Osta Abraham, a Tunisian Jew who settled in Egypt and who also signed his work. However, I have not seen any piece of Siwan jewelry made by Gab Gab that he signed.

11 | The Silversmiths

Master Gab Gab

It is impossible to describe the development of silver jewelry in Siwa without paying tribute to the work of the silversmith Senoussi Daddoum Aani, known as Gab Gab. Senoussi made beautiful jewelry for the women of Siwa and of al-Gara, and has become a significant figure in Siwan cultural history. Although most European travelers who visited Siwa do refer to the jewelry, the seclusion of Siwan women has meant that very little was written about it, or about its remarkable silversmith.

To this day, the inhabitants of Siwa are buzzing with memories and stories about Senoussi. He was clearly an immensely talented, successful, and much respected person, and it is said that every father wanted Senoussi to marry his daughter. He was light-skinned, strong, and a quiet, somewhat complicated, and unconventional man. Senoussi revealed his skills in a variety of enterprises, but his main work at first was as a blacksmith. Siwans say that he was given the nickname Gab Gab because it mimics the sound of the blows of the hammer.

The date of Master Gab Gab's birth is unknown, but he died an old man in 1958. His father was a *fellah* who worked in the gardens, and his two brothers Osman and Hamza were also busily employed in the oasis. Osman made saddles stuffed with palm fiber, and padded shanks for donkey carts. He also made sturdy wooden doors and wooden locks from

75. Blacksmith Muhammad Heda at work.

planks cut from the palm trees, and cut the stones for the rotary grain mills. Hamza, like his father, worked in the gardens.

As a young boy, Gab Gab, like other Siwan boys, helped in the gardens and learned to handle the pruning knife, the *emjir*. Handling the *emjir*, he learned its form and construction, and how these features relate to its use. The impressed decoration on the handle or blade of the tool was the blacksmith's own mark. He most probably learned the secrets of metalworking when he was a child from a relation, or a smith who was glad to train a young boy who showed interest and promise. In Berber society, the craft was traditionally passed from father to son and in this way skills and techniques were perpetuated through the family lineage.

In Siwa, metalsmiths had prestige because the tools they made were crucial to the economy of the oasis. The highly valued *emjir* (meaning 'like my son') that was kept by every family, as well as hoes, rod sickles, and other specialist tools for use in the date and olive gardens, have been made by generations of Siwan metalworkers. They also once forged the swords and spears that were used in the tribal conflicts, alongside the greatly valued European blades made in Toledo in Spain, and Solingen in Germany, that had arrived via the caravan roads from ports on the Mediterranean.

In addition to being skilled in the techniques of metal work, Gab Gab had a mechanical and inventive bent. There are countless stories of his ingenuity and the way he helped to improve the daily life of the

76. A blacksmith
carving his mark on
a pruning tool, *emjir.*

community. He could turn his hand to anything. He could do plumbing,
repair radios, and make wooden wheels. He lit the first street lights in the
town. It is even said that he could turn a stone grain mill by making circles
with his hand above it. He is said to have been involved in the introduction
of the first telephone line linking Siwa and al-Gara with Marsa Matrouh
and the outside world. As a young man, Gab Gab was given the job of
patrolling the high desert tableland from Siwa to al-Gara by camel or
donkey and making any repairs that were necessary.

As modern inventions reached Siwa, Gab Gab was both curious and
interested. He soon mastered the intricacies of the internal combustion
engine, becoming responsible for the repair of the cars of government
officials. When people from outside arrived in the town, they relied on
him to make sure their vehicles were mechanically capable of getting them
home without breaking down. He also owned one of the first cars to enter
Siwa. This vehicle had originally belonged to Captain Hillier, a British
officer in the Frontier Administration who had then become head of the
Libyan Oases Association. But Gab Gab was interested in more than
merely driving a car. He caused sensation after sensation as he took the car

apart and used the engine to drive an olive press and a grain mill, and to raise water to irrigate the land. As he acquired more spare parts, it is said he put the car together again with a wooden cabin and wooden wheels bound with fiber from the palm trees.

Jewelry had been made for the people of Siwa by local metalsmiths for centuries. Gab Gab, assisted by his apprentices, continued this tradition, manufacturing ornaments from the silver coins his customers brought to him and producing pieces that embodied a distinctive style that had evolved through history. This is not to say that there was an unbroken chain of silversmiths in Siwa. In times of political and economic instability, such as during the turbulent years of the nineteenth century, it is likely that craftsmen working in precious metals would flee to safer places where they could make a better living practicing their art. Such a break in tradition, in addition to Gab Gab's inventiveness and the increase in the amount and variety of ceremonial jewelry being made, may account for the common belief in Siwa that he was the originator of Siwan jewelry. The ornaments he fashioned were based on the long established forms and patterns he observed in the old pieces women sent to him to be repaired. Like the metalsmiths before him, he modified designs and added his own innovations, sometimes side-stepping the dictates of tribal tradition and creating his own beautiful designs.

In Siwa, the term *ahdad* for metalsmith covers both the blacksmith's and the silversmith's crafts, and suggests a long association between the two. Gab Gab's workshop produced both silver jewelry and garden implements. The tools he made for the *zaggala* who worked in the palm gardens were in great demand, but people also began to take their jewelry to him for repair. Repairing jewelry introduced Gab Gab to the more refined techniques of working in precious metals and fired his interest in the art and artistry of the silversmith. He was encouraged by his customers who believed he could do anything.

Gab Gab became familiar with the different forms and the intriguing motifs that decorated the jewelry coming into his workshop to be repaired. He also observed, as he became more knowledgeable, the styles and variety of techniques employed in the production of pieces imported from the west and from the Nile Valley. Enameling and filigree, which are common techniques across North Africa, were not practiced by Gab Gab, though attempts were made in Siwa to enamel silver. He developed an exceptional skill in engraving, and his representations in pictorial form and pattern of the natural world around him reflect his amazing talents in draftsmanship

77. A Model T Ford driving down a track in Siwa (1930s). *Royal Geographical Society.*

and artistic expression. He lavished remarkable creative invention and technical skill on the small surfaces of the bezels of rings. Rings, of course, took less silver and were ordered continuously.

Master Gab Gab was assisted by two apprentices, and often by members of his family, including his wife, his mother, and his daughter Salma. His granddaughter would tell her own grandchildren how she used to work the bellows to swell the temperature of the fire in the silversmith's hearth. On one memorable occasion, I was there when Gab Gab's heavy hearth *(tabliya)* was carried in to give her stories an authentic aura and zest.

Neighbors and clients visited the workshop, though people say Gab Gab preferred to work without distraction. And besides, the flames, sparks, and working with molten metal made it a dangerous place for mere onlookers. When women were working alongside Gab Gab, men would keep away.

Mabrouka told me, "All the women of Siwa knew that Gab Gab made jewelry, and they knew how well he made it. It was wonderful stuff. We ran to him, and we wanted more!" The fathers and husbands of the women of al-Gara also bought jewelry from the Siwan workshop because they did not have their own silversmiths and there were Bedouin women who ordered certain pieces. Gab Gab was always busy and in demand. "He worked twenty-four hours a day, and always kept his promise," his granddaughter said. "Both rich and poor bought jewelry from him. For the poor he used a lower grade silver and made a very fair price. For the rich he produced something very special."

Gab Gab made a good living. He built two houses well away from his workshop on a large plot of land. He owned a date garden in which he worked himself. He was surrounded by neighbors and was close to a mosque for daily worship. While he did not become enormously rich, he lived well, and ate well—not least because those who commissioned jewelry from him were expected to send 'breakfast' in the form of food such as chicken and eggs to encourage the silversmiths in their work.

Like the blacksmiths, whose product was essential to the economy of the oasis, the silversmiths' product was an integral part of women's ceremonies and especially the wedding. Working on commission for the brides of Siwa, Gab Gab was conversant not only with the prescribed form

78. Gab Gab made this Bedouin woman's bangles; "they are my heart," she said.

and decoration of each constituent piece in their ensemble of wedding jewelry, but also with its protective significance. This did not mean that his jewelry was static and unchanging: he was influenced by neighboring traditions, particularly those of Libya, which was familiar territory for the Siwans. He was inspired by any exceptional piece of jewelry that entered the oasis from outside as currency in the date trade, and sometimes adapted the new ideas to fit the Siwan style. Innovation also went in the reverse direction. People say that travelers from the west were surprised when they saw the quality of Gab Gab's jewelry and they sometimes bought it and took it away.

The silversmith's skills and creativity were rewarded through the recognition and respect he earned from both young and old in the community, but, because of the seclusion of women, he was excluded from the marvelous spectacle of the wedding when the bride and all the guests were decked out in silver jewelry from his workshop. He did see his own family abundantly bedecked in the whole configuration of his ornaments, as they were meant to be displayed. Mabrouka told me that his wife, who was "pale and quite stout," wore a great deal of silver on these occasions: "Gab Gab's wife was covered in it," she said, "and it was the very best!"

79. A wedding ring with eight-pointed star made by Gab Gab.

The orders Gab Gab received were not always for new ornaments. Occasionally, they were to remodel an existing piece. But women say that it was not common for him to be asked to melt down an older item and produce something new. The jewelry he created was not for the melting pot! When a piece was to be ordered, a woman would first discuss it with her husband. They would not approach Gab Gab directly, but would contact one of the female servants he hired to act as intermediaries. These women were kept busy calling at many houses every day. They were freed slaves, or descendants of slaves, whose cultural background meant that they could speak, and therefore discuss the order, with a man as well as with his wife and daughters. The servant would later return from Gab Gab's workshop with relevant pages of designs for them to choose from. Some of his customers, however, preferred to leave it to him to decide. Even when calligraphy was to be included in a piece, Mabrouka told me, "We might leave Gab Gab to make the choice. And even if a design was selected by the customer from Gab Gab's own pages," she said, "he would make some small changes." The women admired his inventiveness. "These ideas just came out of his head," Mabrouka said.

Master Gab Gab would work out the measurements and weight of the piece that had been ordered and would then calculate how many Egyptian piasters, Spanish dollars, and so forth, would be required. The clients then provided the coins they had been hoarding. The torque and the bangles were heavy items, but women told me Gab Gab constantly received orders for these pieces because all the women wore them.

Two young lads, Ali Bosaed and Muhammad Abugsessa, became Gab Gab's apprentices. Muhammad, who later became his son-in-law, would take over the workshop from Gab Gab when he retired. Ibrahim Jella also worked with Gab Gab, but he was later to become a town crier. At first the apprentices were given simple tasks such as amassing the fuel to feed the fire, working the bellows, and bringing water. And most important of all, they observed the silversmith at work. They learned from him the use of tools, and the capabilities and limits of metals. The silversmiths used a few tools including a crucible in which to melt the metal, hammers and mallets, pliers and tongs, chisels, punches, and engravers. They learned how to make clay molds for casting metal and how to make tools. They forged, hammered, cut, pierced, and punched as they began to master the techniques of metalworking. And they instinctively related some of the well-established forms and patterns they engraved on rings and pendants to the aesthetic and mystical values of their society. They discovered the importance of symmetry, weight, and balance, especially in forging a torque and the large disc that would hang from it.

Minor changes of style were inevitable as the apprentices developed their own skills and techniques, and the older generation of Siwan women can still identify the maker of any piece of their jewelry from the local workshop. The apprentices were well taught by Gab Gab and their work was rated highly by the women who wore their jewelry. These were often the poorer women in the community who could not afford the more prestigious ornaments made by Gab Gab himself.

Muhammad Abugsessa

Master Gab Gab gave up silversmithing after the Second World War, though people say he never really stopped making silver. He was then replaced as Siwa's silversmith by Muhammad Abugsessa. However, the supply of silver coins, the traditional source of silver for the women's jewelry, was beginning to dry up, and silversmiths had to supplement the supply with silver ingots imported from South America.

Muhammad Abugsessa continued to make silver jewelry for the women of Siwa, but problems arose for him in that women of the wealthy families were starting to wear more fashionable gold jewelry bought in the cities, as well as their silver pieces. Transferring the silversmith's techniques to the softer gold metal, in Siwa, was out of the question. Fortunately for him, another demand for his skills arose as the number of motor vehicles in the oasis increased. Muhammad was an excellent mechanic and there were always vehicles waiting to be repaired in the space outside his workshop. He thought he would make a better living repairing them than making jewelry. When he finally put away his tools, the rapport between craftsman and customer, which had sustained and underpinned the jewelry tradition in Siwa, came to an end.

Muhammad Abugsessa died in 1981 in a tragic motor accident.

Master Amin

A silversmith from the coastal city of Alexandria, Master Amin, then stepped in to provide the Siwans with jewelry that resembled their own. He told me, when I met him in his workshop in the Manshiya district of Alexandria, that he had always been familiar with the Siwans' ornaments. His father, with whom he trained from the age of six, had had regular dealings with the Siwans, and when he later moved to his own premises in a nearby neighborhood, he continued to repair their jewelry and to supply them with beads. He said that he had also provided the Siwan silversmiths with jewelry components like silver beads, spherical bells, and chain, to supplement the local supply. Siwans say that Amin paid a visit to the oasis to collect samples of the constituent pieces of the jewelry ensemble, before he began to reproduce the unique designs that Gab Gab had made so well known.

When jewelry ceased to be made in Siwa, Master Amin told me his workshop became a very busy place. On their visits to Alexandria to sell dates and olives, Siwan men would take lists of jewelry items compiled by their wives and daughters and female neighbors for him to supply. This gave him time to fabricate special orders from his stock of chains, engraved plates, perforated metal shapes, spherical bells, glass, stone, and plastic beads, and colored stones set in silver mounts.[74] Master Amin retained the well-established forms and replicated many of the engraved designs, but he also began to incorporate his own innovations, such as covering the surface of the *adrim* with intricate Islamic patterns. He later produced a new *adrim* which embraced the traditional Siwan design, but he rotated the disc so that the cross formed an 'X.'

The Siwans were glad that the bridal ornaments that had always been an essential part of the marriage ceremony were still available to them. They accepted Amin's innovations, and many of the women completed their ensembles with his jewelry, replacing the pieces they lacked with his bright new ornaments. But though these pieces resembled the Siwan, the

80. Tools in Master Amin's workshop in Alexandria.

81. A *Timisnakt* plate and two rings by Master Amin, with (right) an Islamic design.

metal from which they were made was increasingly low in silver content and lacked the beauty and the white luster of silver. It had little intrinsic value, but it was still expensive.

In the past, the women say, they had taken the high quality of their locally made jewelry for granted; now they began to cherish these old pieces. Indeed some, and especially the rich for whom Gab Gab had made his best pieces, were reluctant to wear the new jewelry made in Alexandria, regardless of the fact that their stock of irreplaceable, locally made ornaments was being dispersed among their families. However, the 'newness' of Amin's jewelry, and his innovations, were important to the younger women, and the novelty of acquiring their jewelry from the city also had its appeal.

With additional orders from Siwa, Master Amin's business flourished. However, Siwa was far from Alexandria socially as well as geographically, and the close interaction and understanding that had existed between the Siwan families and their local smiths was no longer in evidence. It was this connection that had brought into being beautiful pieces such as the *adrim*, the *aghraw*, and the *tilakeen* in the past. However, when Siwan women began to choose gold, Amin was affected like other silversmiths making jewelry for women in rural Egypt, and resorted to work such as repairing silver objects and making 'Siwan' jewelry to sell to tourists. In old age, Master Amin continued to visit his workshop. "When the silversmith has no work, he still goes to his workshop every day," he told me.

12 From Silver to Gold

The most significant change that took place in the dress of Siwan women in the last decades of the twentieth century was the replacement of their traditional silver ornaments with modern gold jewelry. During this time, growing prosperity, improved communications, and tourism not only linked the Siwans economically and culturally more closely to the rest of Egypt, but exposed them to the tastes and fashions of the wider world.

As Siwan women became more aware of life outside, the younger ones began to think that the large amounts of silver jewelry they wore on festive occasions was outdated, and that gold *(dahab)* was essential to a modern fashionable image. This trend was accelerated by the visible impact on societies in Saudi Arabia and the Gulf States made by the sudden wealth accrued from rocketing oil revenues in the 1970s. This filled the souqs with gold, and caused the Bedouin to discard their heavy silver ornaments and replace them with light-weight mass-produced gold. All this was visible at first hand to pilgrims from other places, including Siwa, when they saw the gold souqs while on the Hajj in Saudi Arabia.

Siwan women began to sell their silver jewelry to merchants from the silver souqs of Alexandria and Cairo, who found there was a ready market in the outside world for the pieces that had been specially made for the women of Siwa. The marriage disc *(adrim)*, the torque *(aghraw)*, and the

82. Gold signet rings, *zeytouna*, *humusiya* necklaces,
and hoop earings, in a gold shop window.

distinctive, wearable finger rings were especially sought after. With the
proceeds, the Siwans bought gold. As with other inhabitants of rural
Egypt, they wanted only the best 21-karat gold jewelry, for both its
economic and decorative value.

The change to gold metal, which began to take hold in the 1960s and
1970s, coincided with a period of cultural and economic change in the
oasis. Women now preferred to use machine-made goods that were
increasingly imported from the Nile Valley in the home, in contrast to the
time-consuming handcrafted items they made for their own use and for
exchange. Prices for goods and services were rising and there was an
increased demand for Siwa's dates to supply Egypt's need for foodstuffs. As
the oasis was further incorporated into the national system and
'Egyptianized,' the functions of the women's silver jewelry, that had been
integral to ceremonies and everyday life, were being eroded along with
some old values and beliefs.

One consequence of rising prices was an increase in the size of the Siwan marriage payment. In the 1940s, it amounted to 20 to 30 Egyptian pounds. By the beginning of the 1970s it had risen to 150 Egyptian pounds, and brides were demanding the more valuable gold jewelry in addition to the customary clothes and silver ornaments.[75] Thus, when a bride's father went to the gold souq in Alexandria to spend the marriage payment, he carried clear instructions as to what was needed. The women did not want the more ornate and 'frivolous' gold items that seemed alien to them. They preferred pieces that exhibited regular forms, smooth shiny surfaces, and clearly marked motifs that conformed to the familiar pattern of their silver jewelry.

Just as it was customary for all the women to wear the same assembly of silver ornaments so, when they turned to gold, they went for uniformity in the pieces they chose. The gold jewelry comprised a necklace of hollow, rhomboid-shaped gold beads called a *zeytouna* (meaning 'olive') or a necklace of small, round, gold beads called a *humusiya* (meaning 'chickpea'); signet rings; a wide bangle or two, or three narrow bangles with a textured finish; large hoop earrings; and heart-shaped earrings called *alb Shadiya*, 'Heart of Shadiya.' These items are also among the pieces that are popular with Egyptian peasant and working classes.[76] While the wives of rich men would have the important pieces, others (except for the poor) who wanted to wear gold would have earrings and rings at least.

83. Girls wearing 'heart of Shadiya' earrings.

The *zeytouna* necklace is a favorite about which one young woman said to me, "If I'm not wearing the *zeytouna* I feel I'm not wearing gold." Similar rhomboid-shaped gold beads have been worn by women throughout the Middle East and North Africa for centuries. The significance of olives to the Siwans may also endear the piece to the wearer. And the notion that chickpeas in Siwa betoken good luck adds to the popularity of the *humusiya* necklace. The gold heart-shaped *alb Shadiya* earrings resemble in size and form the silver *gingilt* amulet that was incorporated into chains or bead necklaces and could be linked into an earring. Smaller versions of this type are favored by little girls, and even some of the old women wear this type of earring, thus making a connection between the generations. The heart is today, among the young in Siwa, a popular image that symbolizes love and marriage. It is a motif girls have introduced into their henna patterns and depict in their modern embroideries.

Though a girl will begin wearing jewelry in the form of gold earrings when she is a baby, because of the expense, unmarried girls wear very little gold, and restrict themselves to rings and earrings. Even when the family is rich, some girls will resist displaying their wealth and social advantage. A girl who is engaged and has been given a substantial engagement present such as a gold bangle or necklace, will, however, be proud to wear it.

The gold signet ring exhibits a simple square, rectangular, round, or oblong-shaped engraved bezel, and brings to mind the silver rings the women used to wear daily. Its weight and value is also, of course, a factor in its popularity. In a gold shop in Marsa Matrouh, a male assistant with family in Siwa suggested that the signet ring is the particular choice of Siwan women "because it is smooth and strong, and they can knead dough, wash, and clean without any sharp edges catching during housework." However, back in Siwa, I found that women take good care of their gold jewelry, removing their rings to do their chores as they used also to remove their silver rings, and replacing them when they have finished or when they go visiting. But practicality, comfort, and hard-wearing qualities do count in their choice of gold jewelry.

While these few elegant gold jewels are firm favorites, not everybody ignores the more elaborate pieces. For social gatherings diamond-shaped filigree rings are clearly popular. And some of the rich may wear an elaborate ornamental gold *kirdan* necklace that comprises many pendants and chains.

84. A gold shop in Marsa Matrouh.

Needless to say, it took many years for gold to become the dominant form of jewelry because the silver adornment was greatly valued and embedded in Siwan culture and social experience. Silver may have lost its significance and power for the young, but it continued to be worn by their mothers and grandmothers as a familiar enhancement to their lives. And they still insisted on the young women wearing the heavy silver on festive occasions, just as they did in the past. For example when Aziza married, forty years ago, she said she wore the full array of silver for the first three days of her marriage. It was only on the fourth day that she changed to gold. However, when her sister married a few years later, gold had taken hold in the oasis and she wanted to wear only gold on her wedding day. Her future mother-in-law persuaded her, against her will, to wear the silver *suar* bangles until the third day.

Unfortunately, however, the sale of the traditional silver to outsiders has had a negative effect on the preservation of this important aspect of Siwan culture. This is particularly worrisome as some of the pieces purchased by merchants, in the early days, would have been melted down because of their weight and the purity of the silver, with their design and cultural value ignored.

It is a related fact that in Egypt, the value of gold jewelry is generally determined by the karat and the weight and not by the workmanship—only a small percentage of the price is added for that. Almost all of the gold jewelry that is sold in the gold souqs today is made in Egypt, with a small percentage imported, mainly from Italy, Switzerland, and especially India. Goldsmiths manufacture their jewelry from imported gold bars, that are weighed and stamped in Gamaliya in Cairo or in regional assay offices, and from the old or unwanted 21-karat jewelry people from the countryside bring to the gold souqs to sell. Quality is carefully controlled by the inspection of gold shops, the annual checking of jewelers' scales, and the stamping of finished pieces in the assay offices after one or two pieces have been cut and tested to determine the karat.

Today

13 Everyday and Festive Dress

Traditional Clothes

The splendor of the women's silver jewelry was matched by their colorful silk wedding clothes, and enhanced by the simplicity of their blue striped everyday tunics. The standard tunic traditionally worn in Siwa is a generous T-shape, with long, wide sleeves, and a hem that ends below the knee. This is an ancient form that can still be found in other regions of North Africa, especially Tunisia. The style of dress is called *akbir nwasa*—literally, 'the big, wide shirt.' There were three types: The *tde rumi akbir nwasa*, which was for everyday use, had vertical blue stripes. It was made of *rumi* cloth— a sturdy, loose-woven cotton material. The second, smarter version for married women, *tde akbir lihrir*, was made in a closely woven cotton material with a visible sheen. It had vertical green, red, orange, and black stripes. This tunic was worn to weddings and other public occasions and wealthier guests would wear a silk version of it. They were often passed on to a poor relative or neighbor when a woman had a new one for these special occasions, and the voluminous cut would accommodate any figure or stage of pregnancy. The third type of *akbir nwasa* was an everyday tunic made of silk or silky rayon in black or one plain bright color—red, green, yellow, or orange. When making a visit to her friends, a rich woman would display her status in the many layers of clothes she wore, as many as five or six, one on top of the other.

85. A Siwan girl wearing the blue-striped *tde rumi akhbir nwasa* dress with the *aghraw*. Original photogravure, published by Verlag Ernest Wasmuth (1929).

The women wore underneath these tunics beautiful embroidered white cotton trousers called *srawelin khatem*. A bride received a new pair for each of the seven days of the wedding, and she would wear them daily after that. The trousers were very wide at the top and tied with an embroidered tasseled belt (called a *deket*), which slotted through a hem. The legs were narrow from knee to ankle with an embroidered ankle cuff. In earlier times, trousers were worn only by the wives of rich men, copying urban fashions. They might have been looser, following a Turkish fashion for baggy-legged trousers *(shintiyan)*. The narrow-legged Turkish-style trousers (called *sirwal*) were the trend by the end of the nineteenth century. Photos of Siwan married women taken in the first quarter of the twentieth century show them wearing the trousers with fashionable solid-colored, silk-embroidered ankle cuffs that displayed their relative wealth. The trousers became the norm for all the women and have endured until today as festive wear.

All the tunics had a standard, black cotton, embroidered collar, the *atuk*. The collar was square for married women, and V-shaped for girls. The striped cotton materials were woven in Kerdassa, on the outskirts of Cairo, near Giza. Belgrave mentions that in the 1920s, one brother of the family of weaver-merchants who supplied them "has a shop in Siwa, and the others live in Egypt."[77] The blue-striped material for the *tde rumi akbir nwasa* tunic was sold in ten-meter lengths, enough to make three. Because it was expensive and woven in narrow widths, women often economized by using a cheaper plain black material to form the sleeves and sides of a dress. The vertical stripes with a wider stripe down the center front and back, and the black sides and sleeves, created an illusion of slimness even though the garment was very wide. Girls wore striped dresses like their mothers' (or a variant in red stripes).

Men's Clothes

Into the twentieth century men wore a long, white cotton shirt, baggy *sirwal* trousers which were narrow from knee to ankle, and a skull cap, sometimes under a turban. The rich had a red tarboosh with a blue tassel, and wore a *jird*, a long strip of white silk or wool, over the left shoulder and wrapped around the body. Their yellow shoes were imported from the Maghreb or made in the oasis by immigrant leatherworkers from Tripoli. For festivals they appeared in bright-colored flowing silk kaftans that were worn across North Africa, and derived from Turkey.

Today, Siwan men wear a long, loose cotton *gallabiya* with a collar or neckband opening fastened with a button (*zaraar*). Called the *akbir*, it is made in white (for summer) and green, blue, or beige cotton. Underneath, they wear matching *sirwal* trousers that are very wide at the waist and gathered in with a drawstring. Baggy *sirwal* are worn by fishermen on the Mediterranean coast and are widely worn in the Middle East, for instance in Palestine, Lebanon, and Syria.

A government official wears a white *gallabiya* and European trousers in black or brown, sometimes with a matching waistcoat, and a local cloak in black or brown. After a day's work he may relax in traditional thick cotton sateen *sirwal* trousers, in black or mustard.

Women's Dress Today

These days some older Siwan women still wear the traditional striped tunics, but they are not in common use. For everyday wear around the home and for housework the ready-made Egyptian *gallabiya* that is found throughout the country is a popular garment. This inexpensive, loose-fitting, ankle-length dress is made in a wide range of materials, colors, and prints. In summer, materials such as cotton and lightweight synthetic fabrics are favored; in winter, heavier weights made of synthetic fibers like polyester that are strong and quick drying are worn; velvety textures are always popular. Women express their individual taste in their choice of appliqué or machine embroidery *(azume)* around the neckline, and 'new' additions such as collars, cuffs, pockets, and openings fastened with buttons. A modern variant of the *akbir nwasa* dress, made up in an inexpensive material, is also worn at home. While the basic T-shape and the decorated, black square collar have been retained, the *akbir nwasa* is now ankle-length and is made up in contemporary plain and patterned materials. The traditional hand-embroidered collar combines surprisingly well with these modern materials, and makes the new-old dress authentically Siwan. Likewise, women and girls all now wear cotton or stretchy viscose *sirwal* trousers beneath their dresses, in place of the traditional embroidered ones.

Another popular everyday Egyptian garment is a basic folk dress, with a long gathered skirt that falls from a yoked neckline. For more formal events, some older women like to have a 'better dress' made up in this style, and choose soft, silky materials like georgette, cut velvet, and viscose in understated colors and patterns. At weddings these will be worn under black robes.

For special occasions, an *akbir nwasa* dress is the thing to wear, made up in a more luxurious material. A long-sleeved *natiyac* ('narrow dress') is worn underneath the voluminous *akbir nwasa*. This may be a loose-fitting *gallabiya*, a folk dress, or a dress with a fitted bodice and slightly gathered skirt, which is a style favored by younger women and which makes their silhouette bell-shaped. The *akbir nwasa* can be made of a fine semi-transparent material to produce changing color effects, but the *natiyac* is always firmly woven to conceal the body. A woman wearing layers of garments will assemble the colors and textures to harmonize or to contrast. At social events she will be sure to pick up her skirts to display them all.

Whenever she prepares to leave the house to visit friends or relations, a Siwan woman piles on more layers over her indoor clothes: a flowing black 'silk' *akbir nwasa* dress with the standard embroidered square collar, and the Siwan shawl, the *tarfutet*, which will keep her clothes clean and protect them from the dust of the streets. Multiple layers are worn for the sake of modesty as well as appearance and prestige. Wearing layers means a woman can climb more decorously onto her donkey cart, or gather up the skirt of her housedress in order to carry something. She can crouch more comfortably when performing household tasks, such as cleaning rice, preparing vegetables, or making tea on a portable paraffin stove. And her legs will be protected from scratches when she is in the gardens.[78] In winter, the layers provide warmth and in summer are said to air-cool the body.

Girls approaching marriageable age wear clothes that are more fitted to the figure. Though still extending from neck to ankle and wrist, garments follow the lines of the body or are caught in at the waist with a belt. A girl may thus catch the eye of a worthy suitor and make a desirable match. Nevertheless, in the period before marriage it is important to maintain an air of modesty as well as appearing attractive. Ostentatious urban fashions would send out the wrong message entirely. From the time she marries, however, a woman's body shape will be totally hidden by loose layers of clothing. On my last visit to Siwa, I found there was a change to this custom, as girls from the age of thirteen to sixteen are beginning to wear a black Islamic *abaya* with a *niqab* over their Egyptian clothes that covers the entire head and face except for a window for the eyes. A western idea that the veil depicts female submission is quashed by the reasons girls give for wearing this apparel: they say that it is changing their lives in that it gives them freedom to walk in the streets without supervision. One girl said, "Now we can walk anywhere. Before, people would talk. It also earns us respect." Another girl told me that her brother did not like her wearing the *niqab* and some of her friends' fathers or mothers were against it.

Materials, Colors, and Tastes

The Egyptian factory-made *gallabiya*s are easy to obtain, either from Marsa Matrouh, or from a few shops or the Friday souq in Siwa. They can also be bought from women who take them around from house to house, or from a man who travels through the streets on his donkey cart selling Egyptian clothes. A traditional *akbir nwasa* dress, however, will be individually made up by a local dressmaker, by a neighbor, or by the woman herself. The finish of the dress is not felt to be important, though an upper-class woman will expect a higher standard from her seamstress.

Siwan women are interested in and respect the dress materials that are available. There have long been women in the oasis itself who buy bolts of cloth from Marsa Matrouh for that purpose and there is now a shop that stocks a wonderful selection of materials. Women sometimes say that the best and most expensive materials are the dress lengths the pilgrims

86. Fabrics on display in the souq in Marsa Matrouh.

bring back from Saudi Arabia, either as gifts or to sell, and they refer to them as '*moda*'—fashionable.

A woman who is well-off, and able to leave home to take a shopping trip with her husband, may visit shops in the fabric souq in Marsa Matrouh, which stock dress materials Siwans are known to prefer and where they are also known for their good taste and restraint in their choices. There she will find bolts of material in the spectrum of fresh, glowing colors that appeal to the younger Siwan women. There will also be viscose, georgette, and brocaded velvet cloth in browns, greens, and rose-pink for their mothers and grandmothers. On one side of the shop can be found cotton and viscose materials for trousers that are patterned with small flower prints, and there are stretchy animal prints in polyester with Lycra, which were fashionable in Siwa on one of my last visits. On the other, there are rolls of sumptuous black and gold fabrics, and shiny materials imported from the Gulf that are favored by Awlad Ali Bedouin women. Also popular with the Bedouin, though hardly worn by Siwans these days, is red cloth made of any material.

87. A fabric shop in Marsa Matrouh.

The Siwans have clear preferences in relation to colors and materials. Young women today prefer fresh bright colors that mirror the clarity of sunlight—modern hues such as *lemuni* (lemon), *bamba* (pink), *lebeni* (pale blue), and *turkwaz* (turquoise). For festive occasions, rayon damask, which drapes well and does not crease, has long been a favorite to make up the *akbir nwasa* dress. Polyester, striped in one color, is also much used. Fine materials like chiffon, organza, and georgette are frequently machine-embroidered, and light open materials such as silky broderie anglaise and delicate lace are popular. It is hardly surprising that the Siwans, who are accomplished needlewomen, prefer these embroidered modern materials. The embroidery that covers the surfaces also makes them less transparent. There is plenty of choice: Egyptian-made materials that Siwans seem to prefer, and more expensive foreign cloth imported from as far away as the Gulf, East Asia, and Indonesia.

The Siwan woman will expect to spend 300 to 700 Egyptian pounds on a lace dress for *eid*, or 140 Egyptian pounds for a cheaper lace dress to wear at home. When a plain material or, for the sake of economy, an inexpensive one has been chosen for the dress, the purchaser may buy a small amount of a luxurious contrasting material to make bands to insert into the four seams that join the center front and back panels to the sides.

The customer may have the dress made by a dressmaker in the oasis at a cost of 10 to 20 Egyptian pounds, or the shopkeeper can have the Siwan dress made up for her, but it will be incomplete, with the final touches left to the woman herself. The fold across the shoulders will be left uncut and unfinished so that the woman can stitch on the embroidered Siwan collar at home. She may embroider a new collar, or unpick and reuse an existing one, or add a collar she has bought new for around 10 Egyptian pounds. It will be adorned with an asymmetrical design in silky rayon thread, in green and picked out with yellow and orange, and framed with a red and green line. Inside the front of the collar there will be concealed a small, 'secret' pocket in which a woman keeps such things as coins, the key to her jewelry box, mastic from Saudi Arabia, or kohl *(tasalt)* for outlining her eyes.

Another custom is to set two decorated patches of expensive, hand-woven striped cloth into the side seams at the hem, called *litshinab nagil il harir*. Traditionally, these were embroidered with motifs that included a hand for protection from the evil eye, and appliquéd with mother-of-pearl buttons. Now, young women are embellishing the striped material with 'foreign' designs stitched with sequins, pearls, and glass and plastic beads, and latterly with a luxurious decoration with beaded dangles that somewhat resembles jewelry. The patches are also being made larger to accommodate the ornamentation, depending on the wishes of the wearer.

The trimmings encourage creativity and new techniques, and provide relief from the routine of everyday life in their remote oasis. A range of colored yarns, ribbons, braids, lace, sequins, beads, and plastic novelties are now available in Siwa, which women use for the embellishment both of their own clothes and items they make for tourists. Trimmings are also used to ensure that their young girls are well turned out on festive occasions. When I first went to stay in Siwa, it was a fashion for little girls to wear a ribbon rosette with a bead decoration, or charm, attached to the bodice of their round-necked party dresses. At a recent wedding, many were wearing collars, cuffs, and buttons made in luxurious, contrasting materials, like brocade, velvet, or fake fur, and the size of those parts was exaggerated.

Head Coverings

Whether at home or outdoors, women cover their hair with a headshawl *(shal)* that is wrapped snugly around the head, framing the face, and crossed over and covering the shoulders. In summer, it will be made of light, airy materials; in winter, heavier weights are used and lacy knitted shawls are popular. On my last visit to Siwa, in winter, many older women were cozily wrapped in thick glittery headshawls, all crochet *(tignikt nashral)* work by local girls and bought in the souq. The *shal* can be an inexpensive fashion item, and every time I visit Siwa I notice changes in the materials and patterns and in the way young women are wearing it. A large headveil, the *tarha*, may be worn to complement the *akbir nwasa* dress on festive occasions. The head covering for girls is a huge headscarf they pin under the chin, which completely obscures the upper body, or a neat head-wrap they pin and pleat decoratively.

Islam enjoins women to be modest, concealing their ornamentation and physical beauty beneath veils:

And say to the believing women that they should lower their gaze and guard their modesty; that they should not display their beauty and ornaments except what (must ordinarily) appear thereof; that they should draw their veils over their bosoms and not display their beauty except to their husbands [other male relatives are also listed]. Sura 24:31

The *Tarfutet* Shawl

The traditional Siwan shawl, the *tarfutet*, is one of a variety of outdoor coverings worn across North Africa. Wrapped in the shawl so that it covers her from head to toe, a woman's face, head, and body are totally screened from male attention and protected from dust and the glare of the sun. The *tarfutet* has been woven for hundreds of years in the village of Kerdassa, east of the Giza pyramids, and transported to Siwa. It is a large, rectangular sheet of blue and white checkered cotton with blue striped borders. Cotton yarn for the shawl was dyed indigo (obtained from the shrub *indigofera tinctora*) in a dyer's workshop, probably in nearby Giza. The natural dye was likely replaced by aniline dye early in the twentieth century.[79] The *tarfutet* measures approximately 2.10 by 1.74 meters.

A woman receives her new *tarfutet* in two halves which she then sews together by hand. Across the join in the middle of her shawl she will stitch, using silky rayon thread, a narrow band of colored stripes. In a mirror image on either side of the band, she will then begin to embroider decorative motifs such as the hand, the sun, a rectangle, and a fish. In the past there were rules about the placement of a motif and which motifs must be put next to it, but now women can be more creative. The embroidery, called *taksart achtar*, will be worn across her back. She will also work a short strip (*kushit*) with the addition of a protective hand motif or eight-pointed star which she will wear against her forehead, and another strip to wear at her heel. According to social convention older women wear the *tarfutet* without any embroidery or with only the narrow line of stitching across the center.

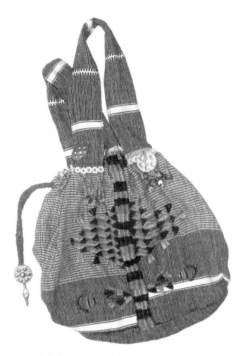

This outdoor cover, which is visible to all, expresses their membership in the Berber group. The Siwans have resisted decorating it with new designs and materials and vivid hues such as they often use now to embellish their festive *troket* headshawl, but when they stitch their lovely traditional patterns across their shawl, they have distinct ways of presenting them and making it their own. Every woman's *tarfutet* is personal and unique, and though they are all competent needlewomen, they have different levels of skill and creativity. A friend can be recognized in the street by the needlework, even though her face is covered. For visitors to the oasis, it is a treat to see the Siwan shawl being worn, its border draped and held at the front, and the colorful embroidery adding interest along the back.

88. A bag made with *tarfutet* material for sale to tourists.

Across North Africa, the Berber Ait Khabbash women who live in and about the palm-covered oasis of Tafilalet in southeastern Morocco, on a trading route that crossed the Maghreb to Egypt, wear a headshawl of similar composition. In photos taken in the 1930s, Cynthia Becker tells us a woman's indigo shawl (called *tahruyt*) was decorated with a line of stitching called *tanammast* joining the two halves of the shawl. By the 1970s, wide bands of wool embroidery that seemed to "create a fertile landscape covered with vegetation" unfurled symetrically either side of this central line and the color palette had expanded to include shades such as fluorescent yellow and purple.[80] Siwan women would recognize the narrow band of colors along the central joining line, and understand both the modern color palette and the new patterns made with lines, curves, triangles, and zigzags.

The Siwan *tarfutet* shawl can be used for other purposes as well. For example, when a woman goes to her family's date garden with her children to enjoy a green and shady place, she is careful to leave it at the entrance so that men will know she is there and will keep away. During the Hajj in Mecca, Siwans use the *tarfutet* to distinguish their tents.[81]

This outdoor shawl is now an expensive item. In 2008, I found the best quality ones would cost 220 Egyptian pounds. Cheaper versions for the less well off or for tourists were a little more than half that price.

The Kerdassa Weavers

There are three workshops in Kerdassa producing the *tarfutet* for the women of Siwa. Muhammad Said Eissa showed me around his family's workshop where the male weavers were hard at work. Two men were weaving the *tarfutet*. The most experienced weavers are assigned to this work and take pride in it; one told me that he had been weaving for fifty years.

A striped cotton and viscose material that was similar to the design of the cloth used for the Siwan *tde akbir lihrir* dress was being woven on another loom. Muhammad told me that this would be exported to Libya. I remember my surprise when a very knowledgeable elderly Siwan, who knew the materials for her striped tunics came from Kerdassa, told me she thought the cloth for the *akbir lihrir* may have come from Libya. The striped design probably entered the Siwan dress code through imitation and exchange between the Siwans and their Libyan neighbors with whom they had close relations. Colorful striped 'artificial silk' shawls in red and yellow were also being woven: on one loom for Benghazi and another for Jalo.

89. Weaving the *tarfutet* shawl in Kerdassa. Striped cotton and viscose material to export to Libya was being woven on another loom.

90. Weaving the *tarfutet* on a four-shaft counterbalance loom.

In the family's shop, Beit Eissa, a few doors down, the salesperson told me that, "Siwan family members or merchants arrive to buy the pieces for the traditional shawl to take back to the oasis." He said, "The Siwans would even refuse the cloth if the line along the edge was not exactly the right shades of red and yellow." He also said that the best weavers would be confident that when a Siwan woman stitched the two pieces of her shawl together, the lines in the cloth would meet exactly. The shop sells hand-embroidered dresses for everyday or festive wear that were made in Sinai, using the black cloth that is regularly sent to them from Kerdassa. "Egyptian women and people from the Arab Gulf buy them. They also like a modern version of the Siwan striped shawl *(nakbir il harir)* that is embroidered and luxuriously decorated with sequins, crystals, and pearls."

In another shop where the base material for the *tarfutet* is purchased, there are shelves with neatly stacked bolts of dress materials, and lining a wall there are mannequins clothed in smart *gallabiya*s patterned with machine embroidery and appliqué. The owner of the shop, Mustapha Hudeib, told me that his Siwan shawls are made in the workshop which takes his father's name, Ismail Abdel-Masoud Hudeib. The cloth is highly prized by Siwan women and is the most expensive of all. Mustapha said,

"It can be made by an old man and not just by anybody." Its production stretches back in time and he believes that his family may once have been the only weavers making the material for the *tarfutet*. Indeed, in the 1920s, Belgrave wrote, "All the material for the women's clothes is made by one family of Egyptian merchants at Kerdassa, near the Pyramids—owing to this the price of clothing is very great."[82]

Mustapha continued, "The material for the *tarfutet* is made from the best quality cotton. Indigo was once used to dye the thread, today a cristal dye from Germany is used at a large sum for Egyptians of 300 Egyptian pounds for one kilo." Mustapha said the shawl is made exclusively for the Siwans. Only occasionally an elderly Egyptian woman will take a fancy to it and buy it. With the embroidery, which Mustapha says he likes very much, the *tarfutet* will sell for about 300 Egyptian pounds.

The *Troket*

When young married women attend weddings and other celebrations, some will wear a spectacular black headshawl, called a *troket*, that is decorated with traditional embroidery and mother-of-pearl buttons. They wear the *troket* thrown loosely over the *shal* so that the shiny embroidery and buttons can be seen to the best advantage. However, they may later remove the *troket* and fold it over their knees, because the weight of the buttons makes it difficult to wear for long.

A girl wears the *troket* the first time at her wedding. It is made of acetate/viscose voile, and sometimes now of polyester. It is adorned with unbroken lines of decorative stitching alternating with lines of equally spaced little motifs. A feature of the shawl is the varying widths of the continuous lines. One narrow line of running stitches with cross stitches over, which is divided into equal spaces of color, is referred to as *tchukabuk* (chattering). A Siwan friend refers to another band of embroidery that is wider and more elaborate as *salam* (greetings), though this may be her own name for it. The linear form, equal spacing, and repetition of motifs seem to echo the pattern of their speech and conversation. The deck, repetition, and balance of motifs that embellish North African textiles have been identified with an oral background in that they seem to reflect the rhythm of the language in poetry and song, the recitation of verses from the Qur'an, and prayers.[83]

When a woman embroiders a *troket* she stitches the lines very straight without needing guidelines. Her work is made easier when there are stripes in the black voile. The motifs she stitches reflect the Siwan way of life and old and present beliefs. They include cosmological motifs—the sun, star, and crescent moon; protective motifs like the hand, seal, and sword; motifs from the natural world—water, represented as an undulating line, the water insect, fish, bird, palm tree, and date; everyday domestic and farming articles such as a drinking glass, comb, scissors, bucket, garden knife, and lantern; and mosques, which denote their religion. The colors of the embroidery are derived from the natural environment—the sun, and the ripening fruits of the date palms and olive trees. The woman works the colors in a set order, beginning with the parts of the patterns that must be red. She then re-threads her needle and adds the green parts of the design. Then she does the same with orange and the design is complete when she adds the yellow and black. When stitching a continuous line made of stripes of color she works them in this order, but puts black or occasionally deep blue between the strong bright orange and yellow. The motifs too are worked with the bright colors juxtaposed to the deeper ones. The colors merge and appear to radiate light across the dark surface.

She makes long, thick tassels *(tishusheet)* from the colored silks and stitches them along three sides of the shawl. She provides a bright contrast to the embroidery by introducing white tassels next to black or deep blue, and yellow next to blue. Some women prefer instead to use for the tassels a collection of electric orange, red, blue, green, pink, and purple colors in acrylic thread that looks like wool. There are trends in the style of the tassels and currently there are some that look like thick ringlets.

The women classify the shawls by the number of lines that decorate them. For example, 'number 47' is the most popular shawl at present. It is also the biggest. There is also a 'number 37' and a 'number 32.' Previously, there was a 'number 60,' and old ladies remember a time when there was a 'number 3' and a 'number 5.' There was a black silk shawl, the *emendal*, which was quite plain except for an embroidered border. Women might have thirty of these headshawls, or even more, and continue to wear them into old age.

When Siwan women embroider bands of tiny pictures over the *troket*, they are not only representing natural phenomena and the objects that surround them in their daily lives, but are reproducing signs inherited from their ancestors. Ancient symbols such as the eight-pointed star, the solar disc, and palms, which are images of regeneration, still speak to the women of their relationship with the environment and rhythms of life. The range of motifs has never, however, been fixed. Through the passage of time, some have emerged or been lost while others have been reinterpreted, given new names, and gathered layers of meaning.

Embroidery Motifs

 amuzdig - mosque

 fanus - lantern

 furs - hand

 gardal - bucket

 khatem - seal

 kubaya(at) - drinking glass(es)

 lebrik - water jug

 nachury - 'to fill up' (pattern)

 taziri - crescent moon

 tajlust - spider

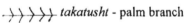 *takatusht* - palm branch

 tamshit - comb

 *tarust* - bride

 tarust we hamisa - 'bride' and 'five' (hand)

 tchukabuk - 'chattering' (pattern)

 tfukt - sun

 timitas - scissors

 tismikt - fish

 tizaret - broom

 ufa - garden basket

 wajj - bird

 warda al arusa - bride's flowers

14 Wedding Costumes

It is hardly surprising that the most elaborate of Siwan dresses are those worn by a bride. Luxurious display is fundamental to the wedding. Before the 1980s, on the first and seventh days of the wedding, a bride would wear a richly colorful silk wedding tunic called *akbir lihrir*, which was green with red, orange, and black stripes, and had the customary black, embroidered square collar. This was always used in combination with a red striped silk tunic underneath. These days, however, a European-style white wedding dress and veil has replaced the traditional wedding costume. Indeed, as the desire for modernity took hold in Siwa, white became the color for a bride to wear during the wedding week, and the colorful striped tunics were gradually stored away or sold to tourists. This was associated with another change, since the growing popularity of gold jewelry over traditional hand-wrought silver stimulated a demand for equally fashionable clothes. The white wedding dress satisfied this need exactly.

The European-style wedding dress was first adopted by the wealthy and fashionable in Cairo in the 1920s and 1930s, and the notion that Western fashions were a symbol of glamour and success was propagated throughout the Arab world through the highly popular Egyptian film industry. One consequence was that the white wedding dress, with all its associations of sophistication and modernity, eventually became a familiar and desirable item throughout the region, reaching Siwa in the 1980s. The modern wedding gown is easy to obtain, but the Siwan bride may receive it only the day before it is needed. It can be rented from one of the women in the oasis who specialize in such things, borrowed from a sister or cousin, purchased inexpensively in Marsa Matrouh, or made by a dressmaker in the oasis. For most brides, the fact that this modern dress is used for only one day, the first day of the wedding, means that it does not justify any large expenditure.

Siwan wedding dresses are not exclusively white, but, accepting white as a glamorous color for weddings, they have blended modernity with their own customs, wearing the traditional embroidered white tunic called *asherah nauak* on other wedding days. For example, on the second day, for the *arak n'tishka* ceremony in which the bride's feet are washed by an old woman (this used to take place on the third day), the bride wears this garment, which is adorned with a colorful sunburst design and decorated with mother-of-pearl buttons covering the front. She wears this again on the seventh day, the *shemata*, when female relations and all the women who have helped with the wedding arrive for a party in her new home. A week after the *shemata*, it is the custom to have a special meal for close relatives in the newly married couple's home. For this, the bride used to wear a silky black tunic embellished in the same traditional style and colors. This is the *asherah hawak azdhaf*—'the decorated black one that makes us happy!' After the wedding it was the custom for her to wear the black tunic when visiting close friends and relatives. Today she may wear the traditional striped *tde akbir lihrir* with black side panels.

These white and black wedding tunics are highly prized and cherished. They are dramatic in their effect, both being lavishly embroidered and embellished with shimmering pearl buttons. Though they are similar in shape, the white tunic has narrow panels of black material let into the four seams that join the sides to the center front and back. The embroidery shows up best on the white tunic, but the rich colors and mother-of-pearl are stunning against the black background.

Beneath these garments the bride wears the embroidered white cotton *sirwal* trousers called *srawelin khatem*. The embroidery that adorns the trousers is displayed below the hem of the tunic so it starts just below the knee. Dotted lines interspersed with tiny solar motifs from knee to ankle cuff cleverly imitate the sparkle of bright sunlight. A line of embroidery also decorates, and strengthens, the lower-leg seam. The cuff around the ankle is colorfully and densely stitched so that it will be noticed. It displays a bold geometric design of squares (called *khatem*) each incorporating eight triangles, and is so clearly marked out into sections that it resembles

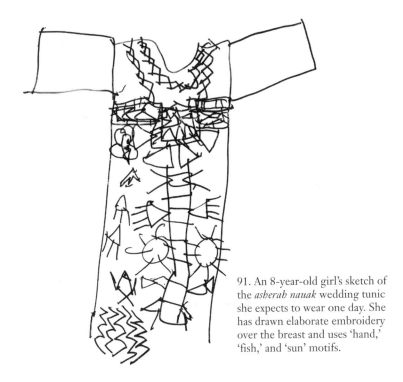

91. An 8-year-old girl's sketch of the *asherah nauak* wedding tunic she expects to wear one day. She has drawn elaborate embroidery over the breast and uses 'hand,' 'fish,' and 'sun' motifs.

appliqué work (i.e., fabric shapes applied to a base material), which is a common technique used throughout Africa.

The bride's traditional embroidered, red goatskin wedding shoes *(zrabin)* have a long tongue at front and back. They were made by Bedouin in Marsa Matrouh for their own people, and there was once a Libyan craftsman in the oasis making them. The soft leather is embroidered with a geometric design of small triangles. The stitch resembles fishbone stitch but lines of thread underneath suggest it is overlapping straight stitch. Around the edge of the shoe is surface cord stitch.[84] These attractive shoes are no longer worn by brides but can be seen in the Siwa House Museum, and in the tourist shops where women sometimes send them to be sold.

A colorful accessory to the wedding costume is an embroidered red leather kohl pot *(tangkult)* embellished with mother-of-pearl buttons and colored sequins. The leather encases a twenty-centimeter length of bamboo that contains the kohl. Its conical leather stopper is attached to a leather handle. A large brass or silver wand *(meruid)* to apply the kohl fits into a compartment at the side of the tube. Leather tassels and plaited rayon 'silk' ropes are suspended from the base of the tube. These days, the *tangkult* is largely symbolic, and after the wedding, a bride is more likely to use a small metal kohl pot, likely from Saudi Arabia. The *tangkult* will be a treasured souvenir of her wedding, and may be hung on a wall to decorate her house. Her mother, though, may still be using the one she received when she married.

The Embroidered Wedding Tunics

Preparations for a Siwan wedding take place well in advance. Indeed, a mother will normally acquire the expensive black and white rayon damask or silky synthetic materials for her daughter's traditional wedding tunics when the girl is about three or four years old. Likewise, she will save for and collect, over a long period, the mother-of-pearl buttons, cowrie shells, and silver charms she will need to decorate the front. The back will be left plain except for the neckline. She will line the front with a fabric such as cotton to make it strong enough to accept the heavy embellishment. The embroidery will be in the five Siwan shades of red, green, orange, yellow, and black. The stitches she uses comprise chain stitch, couching, Roman stitch, a composite of running stitch with crosses over, buttonhole stitch, and fly stitch.[85] It will be the finest work she ever produces.

The embroidery and embellishments reflect her skill as a needlewoman and her devotion to her daughter. They express her desire for the girl's happiness and fertility, and they incorporate elements to protect her from the envious gaze that might be attracted by the impeccable stitching, the gleam of mother-of-pearl buttons, the shine of her gold jewelry, and her glowing good looks.

The embroidery that adorns the wedding tunic of one Siwan girl I met, Warda, is exquisite. Her mother, Haleema, told me it took her twenty years to complete. In truth, it had been intended for Warda's elder sister, who married when she was eighteen, but the stitching was so finely done and took so long that Warda was the lucky recipient when she became a bride four years later! When not in use, the precious wedding garments, or embroidery in progress, are wrapped away in white cloths to keep them clean. It was a privilege to be shown this spectacular dress, which was not for everyone's eyes.

The neckline of the black and white wedding tunics is slit almost to the waist, and the opening is thickly 'braided' with embroidered stripes. Positioned around the opening there are seven square motifs, each divided into four (or sometimes eight) triangles. This motif is called *khatem*, which means 'seal.' The square at the base of the neckline is the largest and most richly embroidered. The placement of the densely embroidered panel over the breast and reproductive area of the body, and the protective sharp corners of the triangles, seem to reveal concerns for the fertility of the bride. From the intricately worked bodice, lines of tiny embroidered motifs radiate over the skirt like the rays of the sun. Many of these symbols such as the hand, sun, eight-pointed star, fish, and water pertain to fertility and protection.

The neckline opening is fastened with mother-of-pearl buttons. The square motifs of the frontal panel (plastron) also are embellished with large mother-of-pearl buttons. Smaller buttons define the sunburst pattern over the skirt, and are arranged in clusters of three, five, or seven—numbers that hold connotations of good fortune and protection. Women say that 60 to 120 buttons are required to embellish a dress, and a girl from a wealthy family will have more. They will be white and lustrous and of the highest quality. Whether she is rich or poor a woman making a tunic for a bride will avoid using blemished buttons or those made of the wrong kind of shell. I discovered this early on when I thoughtlessly collected an assortment of mother-of-pearl buttons in England for Siwan friends and, only when back in the oasis, noticed the qualities I should have been looking for.

We cannot say when the Siwans were first inspired to embellish their wedding clothes with mother-of-pearl shapes, or with the white pearl buttons they call *tutintfukt*—'eye of the sun.' From the middle of the nineteenth century, mother-of-pearl buttons were manufactured in huge quantities in Europe and exported around the world. The creative Siwan women would have delighted in their decorative character and admired their beautiful iridescence that seems to capture the light and energy of the sun.

Buttons are cut from the nacreous, the glowing mother-of-pearl lining, of shell such as the *Pinctada maxima* gold-lipped pearl oyster of Indonesia and the Philippines, which is flat and can be as big as a dinner plate, and many buttons can be cut from it. For centuries, the pearl oyster *Pinctada margaritifera* from the Arabian Sea and the Indian Ocean was carried to the Mediterranean and Red Sea coasts, and taken along the caravan routes for the shell to be carved by craftsmen into marvelous objects of status. Mother-of-pearl, or nacre (from Arabic *naqara*), owes its iridescence to the refraction of light through layers of nacre.

The bride's mother will add an assortment of small decorative objects to the mother-of-pearl embellishment of the tunic, such as: silver charms; plastic amulets like horseshoes and horns; a figure of a little boy to bring the bride good fortune and fertility (and hopefully male children); a tiny vessel shaped like an amphora, which a woman told me would ensure a good supply of mother's milk; and colored sequins shaped like fishes, leaves, flowers, and seashells. (Despite Siwa's distance from the sea, shells are familiar objects. They are often brought back from Marsa Matrouh or Alexandria, and shell fossils also are collected on picnics from several places in the Siwa area.) As an extra precaution, the woman will stitch small silk or cotton cloth bags filled with black cumin around the seventh square at the base of the neckline, and she may attach a large cowrie shell to the square to protect the girl's fertility.

When a wealthy family employs professional help to make their bride's embroidered clothes, this will not be done by one person alone. Instead, one woman will cut out and embroider the dress, and another will stitch on the buttons—at great speed! The bride's mother will have purchased the buttons at the cost of about 150 Egyptian pounds, in recent years from within the oasis as well as from the cities.

An important component of the garment is a pair of detachable tasseled ropes called *gutan* that are fixed either side of the neckline. The *gutan* are plaited using a mixture of the traditional range of colored silks, but appear red. They are decorated with mother-of-pearl buttons, cowrie shells, and sequins and plastic charms in the shapes of shells, horns, fishes, and horseshoes. *Gutan*, described to me by elderly Siwans as a very old and important decoration, are still worn by brides today as an adornment that adds richness to the dress, brings good luck, and supports the girl's desire to be fertile.

92. An old marriage *senduq* decorated with water jugs.

Western Desert Oases Dresses

The embroidered wedding dresses that can be found in the other oases of the Western Desert have elements in common with one another. They may vary in detail from oasis to oasis, and even from village to village, but there are recognizable similarities.[86] The traditional Siwan wedding tunics, however, are unique both in Egypt and North Africa. They are, for example, T-shaped, wide, and straight-sided with long, full sleeves, while those of Kharga, Dakhla, Farafra, and Bahariya follow a wide A-line and have narrow sleeves, similar to styles worn by Bedouin in other regions of Egypt. The traditional Siwan tunics also end below the knee, whereas those made in the other oases of the Western Desert are longer. The fabric they are made of is different as well: in Siwa they are in silky damask, while the wedding dresses from the other oases are in black cotton.

The decoration, too, is quite different: a common feature of the other oases is dense cross-stitch embroidery decorating a panel around a slit neckline, and over the lower part of the back of the dress which shows beneath the veil, and embroidered stripes over the sides and sleeves. Whereas the Siwans used silk and now silky rayon embroidery thread, women in the other oases use cotton thread. Each oasis also has its own favored color combination. The Siwans use five colors: red, yellow, orange, green, and black, which are colors favored for making textiles across the Maghreb. (They also may use a small amount of blue.) Kharga uses red with some purple and blue, and Dakhla and Bahariya prefer red and yellow. Bahariya utilizes a wider variety of colors; this has been variously attributed to the proximity of Cairo with its supply of dyed yarns, or to the influence of people of Siwan origin in the oasis.[87]

Another important difference is the use of mother-of-pearl. While Siwan tunics are decked with mother-of-pearl buttons, the other oases of the Western Desert use silver and imitation coins, and some use a few mother-of-pearl buttons. In the traditional dresses of Dakhla an amulet such as a little fabric pad with Qur'anic verses written inside or a small blue stone to ward off the evil eye may be incorporated into the decoration.[88] The fact that the embellishment of the Siwan tunics is dominated by mother-of-pearl buttons, and that silk materials and silk thread were traditionally used, seems to show the comparative prosperity of Siwa resulting from its flourishing dates and olives trade.

15 The Wedding:
Betrothal, Trousseau, and Marriage Payment

Marriage is the most important event in the life of a young Siwan. It is exciting for the whole community, and the oasis buzzes with news about the latest *arous* and *arousa*—bridegroom and bride. In addition to making a bond between two individuals, marriage strengthens existing family ties or sets up new alliances with other families. A particularly suitable marriage is seen as one which will match or raise the status of families. A man from the higher strata of the community may sometimes marry a girl of lower status who is beautiful, modest, and from a 'respectable' family. Likewise, a girl from a family of the higher class might marry a man from the lower class if he is seen as being successful in his occupation. The marriage gives the couple standing as full members of the community, with new rights and responsibilities.

Siwans prefer to marry within their own community, although a man may choose to marry a girl from Alexandria or Marsa Matrouh, or one who belongs to the Awlad Ali. This, however, is rare, since despite the existence of amicable relations between the Bedouin and the Siwans, the cultural differences are believed to be too great.[89] Siwan men may marry 'outside,' but girls never do unless they find themselves single at the age of twenty. A girl from a large lower-class family, without an adequate trousseau, may find herself in this situation. She may leave the oasis to marry a Bedouin, a relation living in another part of Egypt, or a Libyan from the family of somebody who had lived temporarily in the oasis during the war and married a local girl. She might remain in Siwa and marry a Saidi from Upper Egypt if he has worked in the oasis for some years, and is well known to the community, or another immigrant. Likewise, a girl who leaves Siwa to train as a teacher in Alexandria or Cairo is unlikely to return or marry a Siwan. She may be better educated than any prospective husband, and Siwan custom dictates that married women must not work outside the home.

There is a limited choice of partners in this small community, and informal marriage arrangements have always been made early. Each side will know, or know of, the other family and its background. A boy may become engaged at any time after the age of twelve, but his intended will be a few years younger. This gives the parents the chance to learn more about the young people as they grow up, and to be sure they will be compatible. After that, the boy and girl will only be able to see one another at festivals when he will visit her family and present her with a gift, such as chocolates or a piece of jewelry, at parties in the home, or when the two families arrange to meet in the gardens. If all is well, the parents will meet again when the girl is fifteen or sixteen in order to agree that the childhood engagement should now be formally confirmed. These days the girl can say if she does not wish to marry the man her parents have chosen for her. If the marriage is to go ahead the couple will then meet formally in her home, and the wedding will take place when she is seventeen to eighteen. If she has stayed at school to complete her high-school education it will be when she is eighteen. The bridegroom will be a few years older.

In cases where no arrangement had been made among children, or when the engagement is called off, the mother was usually the matchmaker in finding a bride for her son, and it was the custom for her to make the visit to the mother of a suitable girl to say what she had in mind. Nowadays, the groom's father or uncle will go instead, sometimes accompanied by the prospective bridegroom. The girl's parents will want to ensure that the man has the means to support his wife and children, and that he behaves well. The man's parents will want to know that the girl will adjust to their household and be happy living with them. Though fewer cousins are marrying than in the past, a marriage between them often makes the whole process easier. If a potential bride has been married before, the procedure is different and the initial visit will be made by the man's sisters or cousins or by a professional matchmaker. The prospective bridegroom has to rely on them to answer his questions as he will not be permitted to see his bride unveiled until the day of their marriage.

When the engagement between the young people has been arranged, there may be an engagement party at the house of the bride-to-be. This is a new event in Siwa, though one which the Siwans have assimilated into their own way of doing things. The engagement is celebrated by the female relations after the evening prayers, and after they have visited the bridegroom's mother (who will not be joining them) in her own home. She will have prepared a gift for the girl's family such as a prayer rug and towels. When attending the engagement party, guests take presents like dishes, small glasses for tea, an iron, plastic food containers, and chocolates. The bridegroom-to-be arrives at the girl's house with his brothers or cousins. They are warmly welcomed and given refreshments by the male members of the bride's family. Sounds of the women's merriment and laughter can be heard from another part of the house. In addition to the plain gold engagement ring, the man will have brought with him a gold bangle or necklace and another fancy gold ring. There will also be a bag containing a dress, a headshawl, and some expensive perfume (sinit).

During the evening there will be a special ceremony when, in the presence of the women of his own family, he places the ring on the girl's finger. Some prefer to present the ring in its box. If the man has decided to wear one, she will also put a ring on his finger. About seventy-five percent of Siwan bridegrooms these days wear a ring themselves, most wearing silver following the example of the Prophet.

Some time after the engagement, the groom is obliged to give his bride a marriage payment, the *mahr*, which seals the arrangement and is made to the bride's father about a week before the wedding. In 2008, this was between 3,000 and 4,000 Egyptian pounds: today it is around 6,000. If the woman is divorced she will receive about half the amount. The groom will have been doing extra work in the gardens for years in order to save this money, although his father will help him come up with it. The amount will have been agreed during negotiations between the fathers, and sometimes uncles, of the bride and groom, and the mothers who meet in another room. If the bridegroom wants to build his own house rather than live with his parents, this also will be discussed. When Abdul got engaged, for example, he preferred to live independently of his parents. His father told me he offered to help Abdul build his own house if he would help him in the gardens. "But so far," he admits, wryly, "he hasn't!"

Some of the marriage payment will be used to buy household items such as bedding and kitchen utensils, but the bulk will be spent on gold jewelry. These pieces will be bought by the bride's father in Alexandria, from the 'new' gold shop in Siwa, or from Marsa Matrouh. In Matrouh the gold shops are to be found along the slope of the main street as it leads down to the sea. Most are quite small but they carry a range of the 21-karat gold items that are popular with Siwans, who can usually find what they need there. When the father leaves home to buy the gold he may be accompanied by the bride-to-be, her mother, and her sisters. Sometimes the bridegroom may accompany him. If the bride's father goes alone, he will take with him a list of his daughter's preferences. He will usually be able to accomplish the transaction without much difficulty since the pieces he is buying are established ones, and the shopkeepers are well versed in the Siwans' taste in jewelry.

Popular items bought with the *mahr* are a gold chain and pendant, earrings, and either a wide gold bangle or two or more narrow ones. If the bridegroom is rich there may be a necklace of gold beads or a gold medallion and chain. A small pendant and chain might cost 350 Egyptian pounds (around US$60); four narrow bangles approximately 1,400 Egyptian pounds (around US$250); a filigree ring 110 Egyptian pounds (around US$20); *alb Shadiya* earrings 75 to 200 Egyptian pounds (around US$13 to 35); and a *zeytouna* necklace 1,500 Egyptian pounds (around US$265).

The girl will be delighted with this collection of gold, which is the first significant jewelry she will possess. It shows the commitment and generosity of her fiancé. After the wedding it will enhance her allure in the eyes of her husband, and he will feel a sense of pride when he sees her wearing his gift. At social gatherings it will demonstrate his wealth, and that of his family. The parents of the bride also give her a small amount of jewelry. If her father is rich he may present her with a gold bangle on the morning of the wedding day, or if he is not, with gold rings. Her mother, too, may give her a piece of jewelry from her own collection.

In addition to being decorative, the gold has a practical function as a commodity that will always keep its value and it provides the girl with an asset should she and her husband divorce. In years to come she may decide to sell part of her collection to spend on something else, or to help her husband through a period of hardship; or she may add to her jewelry after a good harvest, electing to use the money she has made through selling embroidery or baskets to the tourists to buy more pieces. If the amount of gold or silver she owns is large, it will be her duty to pay a religious tax, called *zakat*, for the benefit of the poor. Formerly it was paid in kind; now it is paid in cash.

Gold jewelry comprises the most important part of the marriage payment. In addition to the *mahr*, however, the bridegroom will already have given a suitcase containing such items as dresses, dress materials, headshawls, fashionable shoes, and a bag of perfumes, soap, shampoo, and combs at the engagement party. He will also be responsible for providing domestic appliances, in particular a refrigerator. A new trend, imitating other couples in Egypt, is to start married life with ready-made wooden furniture: a double bed, a wardrobe, a mirror, and sometimes a fitted carpet, which he will buy.

The bridegroom's mother will present the bride with a *tarfutet* shawl she has embroidered herself. His family will also send a dress to the bride's mother, further strengthening the ties between the two families. Gifts flow back to the bridegroom's family from the bride's family in the form of a sheep, a basket of vegetables, a sack of rice, a kilo of tea, and some mint. And whenever they visit they will be sure to take something with them, such as sweets and cakes.

The Trousseau

The bride's trousseau of clothes is largely provided by her parents. It will include numerous items for everyday and festive wear, including thirty-five to over one hundred dresses, depending on the parents' income. The quality of the materials as well as the quantity of clothes will be important. The contemporary girl in her modern-day Egyptian clothes will be delighted with her traditional *akbir nwasa* dresses, which will announce her married status. She will have begun to receive them only two months before the wedding to avoid any changes in fashion.

The average trousseau today is likely to comprise:

20–30 special dresses in the *akbir nwasa* style with an embroidered square collar
15–25 *natiyac* (narrow dresses)
1 *akbir lihrir* dress
2 black *akbir nwasa* outdoor dresses, including one of best quality for formal occasions
2 blue-and-white checked *tarfutet* shawls
12 to 15 pairs of trousers
30 headshawls
lingerie
shoes, boots, and sandals

After the wedding the bride will wear the *akbir lihrir* dress whenever she goes out visiting. She will wear it on top of the *akbir nwasa*.

The most prized components of the bride's trousseau will be her traditional wedding dresses. Her mother will have been embroidering these garments since the bride was three or four years of age, and the girl, her aunts, cousins, and neighbors will have helped. A family of high status, however, is always able to ensure that they incorporate the finest embroidery and embellishments, and may employ a professional needlewoman. It will cost about 500 Egyptian pounds to have the *asherah nauak* dress made for a bride.

Of course, the drastic changes to people's lifestyle in the last few years have transformed the wedding, and other ceremonies where the costume was worn, and today fewer embroidered garments are required by a bride. In 2000, a wealthy bride's trousseau would comprise:

2 white *asherah nauak* tunics: one appliquéd with mother-of-pearl buttons and one with cowrie shells
2 black *asherah hawak azdhaf* tunics: one with mother-of-pearl buttons and one without buttons to wear at home
2 detachable tasseled ropes, *gutan*, to pin to the bodice
1 pair of embroidered *srawelin khatem* trousers
7 *troket*s (with long silky tassels in the traditional colors, or tassels in brilliant colors made with synthetic yarn): five embroidered on black cloth, and each embellished with a different material: cowrie shells, mother-of-pearl buttons, fashionable large pearly-white sequins, multi-colored sequins, etc. The sixth would also be black, but without embellishments apart from the embroidery. The seventh, called *nakbir il harir*, is hand-woven with green, black, white, and orange stripes and with less embroidery
1 pair of red, embroidered, goat's-leather shoes or boots, called *zrabin*
1 embroidered leather container for kohl, the *tangkult*
1 finely-made lidded basket *(margunah)* decorated with silk, worsted, mother-of-pearl buttons, and red leather.

With such a large trousseau it looks as if the girl will not need any new *gallabiya*s or festive clothes for a good few years. However, her clothes will get a lot of use and the *gallabiya*s worn for housework, in particular, will soon need to be mended or replaced. She will wear her best clothes at home for three or four months after the wedding, and after that she will use them extensively for visiting and for special occasions. She will wear them for a whole week when she celebrates the return of the pilgrims from Mecca. In addition, fashions in Siwa these days (even colors) are always changing, and young women like to keep up with the latest trends. The girl will therefore alter her clothes to suit the latest fashions. When she can, she will obtain new dresses for her collection.

16 The Wedding: Preparations

There are always red chests being worked on outside the local carpenters' shops, and when one of them disappears it is a sure sign that there is going to be a wedding somewhere in Siwa. The decorated red chest, the *senduq*, together with a smaller wooden box, called the *inhuli*, are given to the bride by her father. Her clothes will be kept in the chest, and her jewelry and other small treasures safely stored away in the box. The chest will provide a link to her family and it will be placed in a prominent position in her marital home.

The *senduq* is decorated on the front with a simple incised and painted design. There are various motifs to choose from, including representations of a water jug, a six-petaled rosette, a date palm tree, and a lion. Two lions holding swords, flanking a large six-petaled rosette, is a popular design. Their ferocity implies protection, and their depiction on the bride's chest is clearly to guard its precious contents. Marriage chests made in Alexandria belonging to some elderly Siwan women exhibit more detailed features, such as a decorated doorway flanked by lions bearing swords beneath elaborate sun motifs.

Everyone is delighted when the *senduq* is brought to the bride's house. I saw this myself when, a few days before Ruqaya's wedding, it was delivered and set down in a small room on the ground floor where the household goods in her trousseau were stacked ready to be taken to her

93. A marriage *senduq* decorated with lions and a six-petaled rosette.

94. A small broom decorated for the bride.

marital home. These included sets of shiny aluminum pans and enormous round trays, crockery, plastic containers and jugs, little glasses, and bedding. Among them were a few homemade items including symbolic 'brooms for the bride' made of palm, their handles decorated with embroidery and beading; and two plastic containers, padded and covered with embroidered and sequined bridal materials to keep the water cool. In the past, during the wedding festivities, the bride would drink water that had first been taken to be blessed by the sheikh of the mosque.

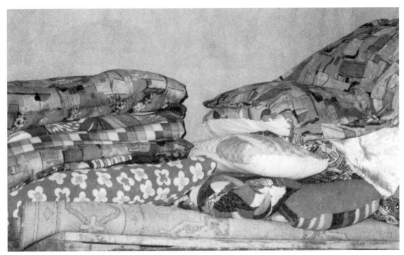

95. Cushions (*shelta*).

Female members of the family had been busy with their preparations for weeks. They had also made new floor cushions for the guests and floor mattresses for relations who would stay over. I once found female members of a family preparing to make cushions for a wedding in their home. The women, who were wearing the traditional short *akbir nwasa* tunic for the task, had fastened their wide trailing sleeves out of the way, gathering them to their shoulders and tying them together at the back of the neck. They sorted through piles of discarded blankets and clothes they had been saving to use as padding, and spread them over the floor. They cut them up into workable shapes, and then basted them together to make the pads. They encased them in hessian, and finally slipped bright print covers over the firm cushions. The whole job took a little over an hour.

The Trousseau Celebration

Up to now the proceedings prior to the wedding have been solely between the two families concerned. Now, the display of the bride's trousseau turns it into a festivity in which the wider community becomes involved. This event announces the wedding, and is the first of the celebrations that take place in the bride's home in the presence of her family, neighbors, and friends. It is an opportunity for guests to reflect on the latest fashions, materials, and colors, and to see the bridegroom's gift of gold jewelry.

I was delighted by my invitation to see the clothes in Ruqaya's trousseau displayed three days before her wedding. About thirty-five

96. The tomb of Sidi
Suleiman: a recent
interior view

women arrived at the house for this ceremony. They had seen Ruqaya
grow up since she was a little girl, and all exhibited the warmest feelings
and excitement for her.

We gathered in a room next to the one where the household goods in
her trousseau were stacked, where Ruqaya was showing them to her
friends. We found places on the bright new floor cushions, which had been
arranged in a wide circle. In the center, Ruqaya's mother Sara was
spreading a blanket over the red-striped kilim that covered the floor.

Sara began to take Ruqaya's dresses one by one from the piles of clothes
by her side, shaking them out and carefully spreading them over the floor.
First, she displayed the festive dresses, made in popular light-weight
materials like lace, silver patterned organdy, georgette, and embroidered
velvet, in modern 'Siwan' colors. There was a striped silk dress that
reminded us of times gone by. They were all in the *akbir nwasa* style with
the square embroidered collar that denotes a married woman. As the
voluminous dresses billowed down, one over the other, she mentioned that
this one had been made by an aunt, or a neighbor had brought the material
from Mecca. Seeing them laid flat, the wide T-shape allowed the textures

and patterns to be fully appreciated. Some of the women were inclined to feel the tactile qualities of open lace or the silky flowers of devore-patterned organdy, to stroke the smooth surface of velvet, or to ponder over the new and opulent beaded panels set into the side hems of *akbir nwasa* dresses—the work of Ruqaya's cousins, or local professionals.

Next Sara showed us the matching *natiyac* dresses that would be worn underneath. They were in the same pure, bright colors, but made from sturdier materials. Some were embellished with machine embroidery, beading, and sequins around the neckline. Ruqaya would wear the most elaborate and expensive of these dresses for family parties, without the overdress. Lastly, Sara displayed, with less ceremony, the headshawls and trousers.

When this first part of the event was accomplished, Sara proudly passed around two red velvet cases containing the bridegroom's gift to Ruqaya: a fashionable gold medallion and chain and a gold bangle, which left no doubt of his wealth and his commitment to her. As they were passed from hand to hand, some women left money on the cases, which customarily helps toward the wedding expenses.

Then came the high point of the occasion: the embroidered wedding garments, flickering with the dazzling reflections of colored sequins and mother-of-pearl buttons, were taken piece by piece from their cloth wrappings and spread over the floor. The white *asherah nauak* dress Sara had made, and the *troket* she and Ruqaya embroidered together, were examined and admired. On the dress, Sara had stitched a new beaded and sequined floral design above the standard traditional embroidery to match that of the *troket*—an innovation which received great interest—though it was clear that some women found the radical new fashion bewildering.

Relatives and aunts, cousins, sisters, and neighbors had given hours of their time and labor, and they were delighted to see their handiwork displayed, whether on a *troket* or the ankle bands of the *srawelin khatem* trousers. In years to come, these precious traditional garments would be a link to Ruqaya's own family and bring treasured memories.

The women helped Sara fold and roll up the clothes and pack them into the red wedding chest, a huge new suitcase, and a new cupboard ready to be taken to her marital home. Because the clothes were made of springy, man-made fibers, or were overlaid with embroidery, buttons, and sequins, they would not crease. In the past a small leather bag would have been placed in the *senduq*, between the folds of material, containing an amulet written on paper by the sheikh from the mosque for the protection of the clothes and the chest itself.

The Henna Night

On the day before a Siwan wedding, *leilat al-henna*, the henna night, which marks the beginning of the wedding, takes place in the home of the bride's family. This comprises the ritual application of henna to the bride's hands, arms, legs, and feet. The day begins with the girl spending time with her best friends. In the morning she showers and it is the custom for her to remove her body hair. On this last day as a single girl with her young friends, she is no doubt reminded that her change of status will bring the company of married women. Meanwhile, female relatives and neighbors come to the house early to help the bride's mother prepare the dough and bake the bread, clean the rice, and get everything ready for the henna celebration and the wedding feast.

In the afternoon about forty girls who are friends and relatives of the bride, smartly and modestly attired in fashions from Marsa Matrouh or Alexandria, gather in high spirits for the henna celebration. It is the last opportunity for them to spend time with her before she becomes a married woman. The joy and happiness they feel for her is clearly tinged with regret that they are in some way losing her.

Before 'the henna' begins, they sit together watching a popular TV program, then dance to *zaggala* and Egyptian music played on a tape recorder. A small, slim girl is the first to stand and dance, from where she sat among her friends, moving her hands slowly and gracefully while rapidly gyrating her hips to the rhythm of drums. Others follow with their own interpretation of the Siwan dance.

The henna ceremony begins when the bride's mother carries in a pile of patterned white enameled bowls. There is one large bowl for the girls who have been enlisted to do the bride's henna and smaller ones for anybody who wants to do their own or a friend's. Four girls, who are well known for their henna skills, have been invited to do the bride's patterns. They first mix the henna powder with tea, a little benzine which will help the marks last longer, and *karkadeh* (an infusion made from hibiscus flowers) 'to improve the color.' The bride's patterns will last quite well because she will not be doing any housework for the first weeks after the wedding. They will be beautiful and assist her wellbeing.

She takes her place on a floor cushion, against the wall, surrounded by her friends. She will stay quite still in this position for about five hours, which is exhausting although pleasurable. On this occasion she is wearing a simple *gallabiya* because her clothes will have to be rolled up while the henna paste is painted on her hands, forearms, feet, and legs to the knees.

The girls who are the henna artists have brought with them sheets of intricately cut plastic floral and leaf stencils. They will combine this technique with traditional patterns drawn using a small stick. They decorate the bride's skin with motifs, and words in Arabic wishing her good fortune and happiness in her marriage. Into the night they stencil a large spray of flowers across her palm, draw small hearts along her fingers, words of love in Arabic on her wrists, and calligraphy and intricate patterns along her arms and legs. There is a message written to her new husband to look after her well.

Halfway through the henna, a dinner of rice and chicken is brought in, and the girls find places around large trays on the floor. The bride's brothers, who were waiting in case anything else was needed from the souq, have been served separately outside. Some of the women, having finished in the kitchen, join the party to see the bride's patterns. If they are not too tired they stay to watch the henna and the dancing into the night.

Preparing the Wedding Feasts

These days the Siwan wedding celebrations take place over two days. Lavish hospitality is fundamental and, with the help of neighbors, friends, and relations, a family puts on the best show possible. They may need to borrow money in advance in order to pay the wedding expenses, repaying it later in cash with the contributions they receive, or by allowing the lender to purchase their dates at a reduced rate at harvest time.

The person responsible for organizing the food for the wedding is the wedding specialist who is also the midwife, the *takadumt*. She will be busy with her duties until the wedding is over. Large amounts of food are purchased or donated, and will be prepared at the homes of the bride and groom. In other houses around Siwa, women bake flat bread, date bread, and batches of bread rolls and large plain cakes that are more recent innovations.

Sheep are sacrificed at sunrise for the feasting. The meat is cut up and prepared and the head and legs are taken into the house to be cooked the following day. The men have a breakfast of *fuul*, stewed dried broad beans, served with bread and honey, and the better-off will have milk and eggs. Then they go to the gardens to collect firewood from olive trees. It is always easy to tell when there is going to be a wedding in Siwa because of the smoke rising into the clear sky from the garden of the bride's house.

For the bride and her family the most important celebration is the one that takes place on the wedding day at their home. It will be attended by their relations, neighbors, and friends all dressed in their wedding finery. The bride, seated in a place of honor, will preside over hours of dancing, singing, and feasting.

The grand feast at the bridegroom's house now takes place on the second day and large numbers of male guests, as many as fifteen hundred, will have been invited to this celebration. The women who offered to do the cooking arrive early in the morning to begin preparing the food before the relentless heat of the fire and the sun begin to impede their work. One will record the names of all those who have helped, so that in the future, when there is a wedding or other function in their homes, their work can be reciprocated.[90] Siwan women are not afraid of work, and those who are given responsibility for directing teams of helpers preparing the food are proud to be chosen, and they run to their pans!

The wedding celebrations, the display of the trousseau, and especially the feasts when hundreds of people are entertained, are a huge drain on the resources of the two families, though offset by a well-established system of reciprocity. Their generosity, and the enjoyment of the guests, will greatly influence the future status of the two families.

17 The Wedding:
Ceremonies

The whole town is included in the Siwan wedding. These days the festivities are focused on the first two days, and resume for a women's celebration on the seventh. On the first, the wedding day, the bride's father, together with the father of the groom, sign the marriage contract in the presence of a government official. At the same time, the bride will be bathing at home and spending time with her best friends. Later, in the home of a woman who is accomplished at beautifying the bride, she will have her hair styled in the presence of other women and will be dressed there in her modern white wedding dress and veil. Her parents will arrive and admire her and congratulate her warmly before she is driven round the town in the first wedding procession, or *zaffa*. Meanwhile, the bridegroom will be taking his bath with his friends in the Cleopatra Spring where they will celebrate and make merry with *zaggala* music in the time-honored way.

Before sunset, the bride with her father or an uncle and one or two of her aunts lead the wedding procession in a car decorated with colored paper and balloons, followed by a column of other vehicles. More recently the bridegroom has been known to join the procession in a separate car, but this is a new trend as he was not previously involved in this ceremony. Trucks loaded with children in their best clothes follow the bride's car slowly past the mosque and through the main square, the drivers honking their horns loudly and the children enthusiastically singing and clapping.

The joyous wedding procession engages the whole town in the wedding, and surprises and delights the tourists who are getting used to the peace of the oasis. The singing is ear-splitting as the procession passes, and fades as the trucks pass off into the distance to the tomb of Sidi Suleiman where it is a custom for the procession to come to a halt to enable the bride to pray for a happy marriage, and that she will have children.

The bridal party then arrives at her parents' home and the wedding celebration begins. It is an exclusively female affair, with the men gathering outside in the garden. Inside, the bride takes the place of honor in a special white-painted chair, sitting on a high cushion so that everyone can see her. She sits under a bower of flowers, and there is a vase of flowers that have been dried under the sand next to her. She sits facing the lively guests, who smile and talk noisily together. A summer wedding is fiercely hot, so on either side of her, two girls fan the bride with huge palm leaf fans. She is ritually silent, dignified, and serious. The party is attended by the bride's female relations, friends, and neighbors, and they are all there, packed into the space beyond her chair: the boisterous little boys; small girls, some with kohl outlining their eyes; older ones, chatty and frilly in broderie anglaise and silks; teenage girls, attractive and shapely though covered from head to neck and wrist to ankle; and young married women in lustrous *akbir nwasa* dresses, some cradling their babies. Older women garbed in black robes, or the *tarfutet*, sit together peacefully chatting in another room throughout the celebration.

When the time comes for serving the food, the bride retires to another room with a small number of aunts and cousins. She may be given some liver to eat. It was customary to serve the bride an egg, perhaps as a symbol of fertility and protection. The guests sit around large trays on the floor and are served chicken or lamb and rice with olives and lemons. There are glimpses of flashing gold bangles beneath wide sleeves, and large hoop earrings sparkle with light when a woman's headshawl slips back from her hair. As one friend said to me, "Women are used to observing one another this way. They will notice every hidden detail. They even notice the trousers!" If it is hot, married women will have knotted the wide sleeves of the *akbir nwasa* dress together at the back of the neck to be cooler, revealing the long narrow sleeves of the plain or print *natiyac* under-dress, and gold bangles if they have them. This also creates another elegant dress style that totally changes the visual appearance of the summer wedding.

The bride returns to her chair to sounds of joy and the loud buzz of conversation and laughter. The room reverberates with the beat of *zaggala*

97. A bride in the white *asherah nauak* tunic.

drums played by a young boy, and a girl's voice soars above it as others join in with traditional Siwan songs. A girl moves into the center of the room, tying a scarf low around her hips as the guests press themselves back against the mud walls to make a space. She begins to move her arms slowly and elegantly in time to rapid hip movements that are reminiscent of belly dancing. The atmosphere is electrifying as the music, the spectacle, and the movement sweep the guests along in a mood of excitement and happiness. At intervals during the evening a woman throws sweets and little gifts from a basket over the floor, and the children and one or two of the women swoop on them headlong.

At around ten o'clock, amid shrill undulating cries of joy—the *zagha-reet*—the guests hurry to line the hallway to see the bride, a thick lace veil now covering her face, quickly leave the house. She is accompanied by her friends who are wearing white dresses and the traditional embroidered trousers. Outside, she steps into a car with her sisters and aunts which leads the procession of cars carrying friends and relations, and the bridegroom's family who are conventionally impatient to take her to her husband. The children on the trucks that follow sing loudly in Arabic, "Zeina, zeina, zeina, waddina al-arusa wa gina"—"Beautiful, beautiful, beautiful girl, we delivered the bride and we went home." Back inside the house the room suddenly feels very hot and we sip water from a huge tin mug that is handed around to the guests before we leave along the moon-lit sandy track.

The bridegroom waits outside his house to welcome his bride, wearing a new white *gallabiya*, and sometimes a prestigious waistcoat and a black-and-white or red-and-white-checked *gutra* around his neck. Paper streamers, sweets, and coins thrown by his friends and relations drift down from the windows and roof of the house as the bride arrives. While the boys in the street scrabble for the treats, the groom takes her hand and they sweep into the house followed by her friends. The couple go into the bridal room and lock the door. After a few minutes, the girls knock on the door, and the bridegroom emerges carrying a gold-plated watch and a handful of banknotes, traditionally 50 Egyptian pounds but now 100. In a ritual called *abesha*, he presents the gift to the wedding organizer who immediately takes it to the bride's mother as a token recognition of the girl's virginity, and of her good influence on her daughter. The wedding organizer in return receives a gift for her role as the person who first gives the bride's mother the good news. To celebrate all this, the women of the groom's family, when he presents the gift to the woman, and the bride's family when her mother receives it, will chant, "Sala wa sallim aleik ya sidi ya rasul Allah"—"And praise to the prophet of Allah"—six or seven times. This 'night of the entering' *(leilat al dukhla)* marks a change in the couple's status from childhood to adulthood.

On the second day of the wedding *(sebait tarust)* the focus of the celebrations moves to the bridegroom's house. At about five or six o'clock in the morning, up to a hundred of the bride's neighbors and relatives gather outside. The bride's sister or cousin knocks on the door as a signal for the bridegroom to leave. Before he goes he throws, from a scarf-wrapped bundle, sweets, fruit, coins, and small gifts such as fancy hair-slides, combs, and shampoo over the floor of the house. The ritual scattering of gifts, the *asenhab*, takes place throughout the days of the wedding and is great fun for everybody.

The bride is wearing the only clothes she brought with her, a special white *akbir nwasa* dress with the square collar that signifies she is now a married woman, with a special white *natiyac* dress underneath, and a fashionable, sparkling *troket*. While her new husband attends early prayers in the mosque and then spends time with his friends in the gardens, she awaits the arrival of the *zaffa* that will bring her marriage chest, dishes, and pans, and all the items of her trousseau. She may also be thinking about her mother who is receiving congratulations from women at home.

At ten o'clock the bride hears the sound of children singing as the trucks approach the house. The town criers and her uncles and aunts and brothers and sisters are all in the procession. In the past, the women would have been adorned in their festive silver for this ceremony. The town criers carry the bride's red chest into the house and her relatives help bring in the rest of the goods. The bride's mother will also have sent incense and food-stuffs: spices, bags of flour and rice, date bread baked the previous day, chick peas for good luck, and some beans for her good health and fertility. It is a tradition to send the bride a basket of dates, which symbolize wealth and fertility. There is a saying that all the items must be returned if the dates are missing. The groom's relations put the things away and find a place for everything.

At noon a small number of the bride's relatives, about seven to ten in all, will gather for the *arak n'tishka*, the 'cleansing the feet' ritual. This is the first day the bride wears her white *asherah nauak* wedding dress, the embroidery illuminated with mother-of-pearl buttons and sprinkled with colored sequins. The other young married women will wear theirs but they will later change clothes to serve the food.

98. A *senduq* in the
Siwa House Museum.

An old woman, possibly her grandmother, washes the bride's hands, legs, and feet, as the girl remains ritually silent, looking down, and still. The water was carried from her mother's house, and probably relates to the fertility and good fortune she is expected to bring into her husband's home and the protection of the couple.[91] After the cleansing ritual, the old woman walks around the sides of the bedroom, symbolically sprinkling water. Throughout the wedding ceremonies it is the custom for the bride to remain silent and immobile,[92] which will assist her in making the emotional journey from her old life as a young girl to her new social position as mature married woman, and to face leaving her own family for the prospect of living with her husband's family.

They share a meal, and the dish called *dishish* is served, which signals the end of the wedding. One of the bride's relations will have brought a purse to give to the bride from her mother containing the watch and money that the bridegroom gave to the wedding organizer the night before, plus a large sum—300 to 500 Egyptian pounds—to which relatives and neighbors contributed and which the girl will give her mother-in-law toward her wedding expenses.

While all this is going on, preparations for the feast for the men later in the afternoon are well underway outside. The street has already filled with male well-wishers, many of whom will have received a wedding invitation. Neighbors open their gardens to accommodate all the men who will stay and eat. The men will contribute about 10 Egyptian pounds (or more if they are affluent or related) toward the wedding expenses. Some families will have donated ingredients such as rice, olive oil, salt, pepper, and soda. Others may have contributed a sheep or a goat. Some lent pans, trays, glasses, or cutlery. A man at the gate collects the money and makes a list of those who will dine. The men, seated in groups of about six on the ground, will share a tray of lamb, goat, camel, or beef with rice and pasta, and pumpkin and other vegetables. The food is washed down with soda, fruit juice, tea, *kerkadeh*, and water carried from the spring.

The final part of the wedding festivities takes place on the seventh day, *shemata*, after sunset when the bride receives between fifty and two hundred women guests in her new home, the number depending on the wealth and status of the two families. They will all have helped in some way to ensure the wedding was a success. Resplendent in her embroidered wedding costume and a hand-woven striped *troket*, the bride's new status is displayed before the guests. Accompanied by young women wearing their traditional wedding clothes, she is visually incorporated into the married group. Her mother is there, specially collected and brought by other women. It is the first time she has seen her daughter in her marital home and of course she feels very proud and happy.

The guests are served drinks such as tea, cocoa, soda, and sherbet, with cookies and sweets. Many guests will have brought some as a contribution. All the women who visit the bride on this occasion take home a bag with fruit such as apples and bananas, sweets, peanuts, chickpeas, and juice. If the family is rich there will be a slice of *gumar*, the precious raw white heart of a palm tree, which, adorned with flowers and money, was earlier presented on a tray by the bride to her mother-in-law.

As well as providing these feasts, the families of both bride and groom will receive visitors who come to say *mabrouk*—congratulations—throughout the period of the wedding. If the bride and groom are from the East, people from the West will go along if they know the families concerned, and vice-versa. Just as the bride does not see her mother, the groom does not see his father until the end of the festivities, an observance that avoids embarrassment regarding the couple's sexual initiation and the transitional stage of their new relationship. During this time of adjustment, the newly married couple will spend the daytime apart, the bridegroom celebrating in the date gardens with his friends, and the bride at home, sitting surrounded by her husband's young relations who entertain her with dancing, singing, and joke-telling. One week after the seventh day *(shemata natnu)*, the young couple will welcome their families to their home for another celebration.

After the Wedding

In the first weeks of marriage and residence with her in-laws, the bride is not expected to do any housework. Every day in the house she wears her gold jewelry and special dresses from her trousseau, which she will change once or twice throughout the day. Wearing her fine clothes and jewelry adds to her prestige in her husband's household, and boosts her confidence in her new position. She is given nutritious foods to eat. She will hope soon to become pregnant; her first pregnancy is especially important because it proves her fertility.

For the first couple of months after the wedding the girl limits her social visits, though she may go out in the tuktuk with her husband, and does not attend public events. Under the wing of her mother-in-law she begins to adapt to the new household and the break from her own family, behaving appropriately as a good wife, respecting and obeying her husband. At the end of this initial period of adjustment to her new life it is the custom for her to 'reconnect' with her parents and return to stay in their home for a week. Her husband marks this event with the gift to his father-in-law of a sheep and other foodstuffs such as vegetables, olive oil, and sugar (if he can afford it), further cementing their relationship and strengthening the alliance between the two families. All the bridegroom's female relations visit her there, taking with them presents of sweets and some money. There is a special meal, and each of the women guests receive a bag of party gifts with fruit and nuts to take home.

At the end of her stay the girl returns to her marital home and normal married life begins. She pays visits, and attends weddings and other public events. Whenever she visits her friends or relations after the wedding, she will take with her a bag with dresses and headshawls to change into and to show off the special clothes in her trousseau. On any first visit, when she prepares to return home before sunset, she will be given small gifts such as sweets, cookies, money, or soap. She wraps them in a corner of her *tarfutet* to take home.

The bride is gradually incorporated into the domestic routine as her mother-in-law assigns duties to her. She will already be good at housework

99. Selling from home.

and know how to make bread, having helped her mother with these tasks from the age of about nine. She shares the household chores with her sisters-in-law, and there may be a rota. Siwan houses are kept clean and tidy, and the girl may be kept very busy and expected to do the housework to her mother-in-law's exacting standards. During the wedding festivities, however, the bride's relatives may have flattered the bridegroom's mother a little and done their best to ensure that she will not expect too much of the young girl. The mother is typically a powerful figure in the home. She is responsible for the smooth running of the household, and also for the behavior of her daughters and daughters-in-law. She can sometimes, therefore, be the cause of unhappiness for the young women. It is not unheard of now for a husband to refuse to allow his young wife to cook or do the washing for his parents. Nevertheless, both parents are greatly respected and well taken care of.

Living in the extended family can of course bring advantages such as sharing child care and the company of other women of the household, but many couples would prefer to have a house of their own. This is difficult because a man is indebted to his father who will have helped pay for his wedding, and may also be supporting his son and his family living in his home, especially if his son works on his land.

18 Winds of Change

In the last decades, this once isolated oasis has been affected by the pressures of rapid change. The new tarmac road from the Mediterranean coast, tourism, television, the tuktuk and motorcycle and greater prosperity have exposed the Siwans to the influences of the wider world and introduced them to new concepts of glamour and fashion. As a result, time-honored rituals have been modified or abandoned; old tastes in clothing and jewelry have changed; and traditional motifs have been replaced, or at least overshadowed, by modern designs.

In so far as these changes mean the disappearance of some of the most remarkable and unique aspects of the cultural heritage of the oasis, they are to be regretted. However, things are never quite so simple. Siwa's culture has never been fixed, and taste in clothes, jewelry, hairstyles, and henna have always been influenced by new ideas and trends. Some of these were carried along the trade routes, others initiated by the well-to-do, and others brought by incomers such as Sudanese and Nigerian slaves who became incorporated into the group. The difference is that, whereas in the past the pace of change was slow, the impact of modernity has been disconcertingly rapid. Exposure to the modern world has provided Siwan women with new ideas that have caught their imagination, just as the demands of outsiders and tourists have given them the opportunity to innovate and to modify time-honored traditions.

The women's dress is an important indicator of tradition and change in the oasis. The embroidered headshawl *troket* is a good example of this. While it has always been a great favorite and a symbol of Siwan culture, in the last few years it has also become a fashion statement among young women. Recent local availability of a vast range of materials for embellishment has provided inspiration for the invention of new patterns and motifs. But the new colored yarns and sparkling decorations are always worked on top of the traditional silk embroidery.

Both the authentic *troket* and the modern versions are popular with tourists and, since they can be easily tucked away in a suitcase or backpack, are much in demand. This has provided both a stimulus and an opportunity for Siwan women, who are proving to be highly inventive in their efforts to catch the tourist's eye. Men working in the handicraft shops in the town told me that Egyptian visitors generally like the new embellishment, whereas tourists from the West such as the Germans and the French prefer the traditional embroidery. Needless to say, visitors are sometimes critical of work that has been speedily and carelessly stitched for a quick return, but it is handmade and individual, and provides the tourist with an inexpensive souvenir of the oasis.

The rectangular form of the *troket* provides an ideal surface on which women and girls can experiment with new techniques, materials, and colors. Flamboyant floral designs, greatly amplified traditional motifs outlined with large pearly-white sequins (which imitate mother-of-pearl buttons but are cheaper), and countless other configurations have been stitched over the surfaces of the women's *troket*s. These lively new patterns completely overshadow the bands of ancestral motifs underneath.

Some of the magical associations assigned to the tiny motifs that lie beneath the new patterns have been forgotten, but some have not. For example, fish, hand, and palm branch motifs continue to have meaning for the women who, despite their enthusiasm for new things, incorporate them into their modern embroideries to ensure well-being and fertility. This combination of the traditional *troket* with modern embellishments can be visually stunning. I saw an example worn at a wedding I attended on my last visit to Siwa that had been made by local professionals. Foreign motifs such as fans, baskets of flowers, and ribbon bows were appliquéd with hundreds of tiny mother-of-pearl buttons, silver sequins, pearls, and crystal beads. In addition, the shawl was hung with silver coins, and pearly-plastic tubular amulet cases decorated with bells (like the ones Gab Gab made in silver) with calligraphic messages written on them such as *alf mabrouk*—congratulations; *marhab il' arusen*—welcome to the bride and groom; *ayamna hilwa saida*—happy days; and *el hamdulilla*—thanks be to God. The delicate traditional embroidery, visible beneath the embellishment, provided no more than a rich texture. This lavish and prestigious variant of the *troket* was worn by only a handful of the guests but was a focus of discreet admiration for the exquisite handiwork.

The nature of the Siwan wedding itself has also been undergoing change. Some families now decide to cut down on the expense and extravagance of entertaining large numbers of guests, and some ceremonies have been either modified or dropped. A few families have brought forward to the first day the *arak'n tishka*, the washing of the feet ritual, when the bride appears for the first time in her embroidered wedding costume. Some have abandoned it altogether. Likewise, in the ceremony called *atras*, the bride's hair is now styled in the fashion of Egyptian brides in the home of a woman professional before she is driven around the town and then home for the wedding party. The *zaffa* procession itself is also made shorter.

The traditional wedding costumes are still greatly cherished, but most brides now limit the garments to one white *asherah nauak* dress, one pair of embroidered *srawelin khatem* trousers, and one or two *troket* headshawls. Their grandmothers would have had as many as thirty *troket*s and, even as late as 2000, a bride would have at least seven. Now, some girls are even asking their parents to give them gold jewelry in place of two of these headshawls when they marry. This is hardly surprising since the decoration of a modern *troket* will very soon be out of fashion, though it was expensive and time-consuming to embroider. At special events after the wedding such as a birth ceremony, when young women traditionally wear the embroidered white *asherah nauak* dress, the simpler white *akbir nwasa* adorned and upgraded with two fashionable beaded panels at the hem is being worn in its place.

A change of greatest significance has been the disappearance of the splendid handcrafted silver ornaments worn by Siwan women and their replacement by factory-produced gold. More extensive exposure to the outside world from the middle of the twentieth century revealed that everywhere gold was the metal of choice for the rich and the fashionable. This inevitably caused a change in the attitude to silver among the young women. It took time for silver's dominance to be undermined, but brides began to demand gold ornaments as part of the marriage payment, and women began to include gold jewelry in the shopping lists they gave to the men when they set off on their journeys to Alexandria or Marsa Matrouh. Indeed, the opening of a gold shop in Siwa was particularly significant in that it meant that women as well as men could become involved in the purchase of gold jewelry. Mr. Ashraf Mohammad, who had a gold shop in Marsa Matrouh, opened the shop in 2000 in a quiet spot in the palm gardens only half a kilometer from the center of town. This meant that a woman could enter in the company of her husband or father and see the gold placed on the scales and weighed, thus becoming involved in the process of purchase. One woman once said to me, "I never went with my husband to Alexandria to buy gold so how could I know what it cost?"

This demand for the new gold jewelry does not, however, mean that the women choose a wide variety of designs. As in the past, they prefer to be seen in the same pieces that are worn by other Siwan women even though their jewelry is now gold rather than silver. Indeed, the owner of the gold shop in Siwa soon adapted his stock to suit this preference in his local customers. A year or two after it opened he confirmed my opinion that certain familiar pieces, in particular the heart-shaped earrings known as *alb Shadiya*, the necklace of olive-shaped gold beads called *zaytouna*s, signet rings, and filigree rings, were clearly the Siwans' favorites. Needless to say, young married women are more adventurous and eager to try out new styles—especially for the less expensive, lighter, and most frequently worn items of jewelry, such as earrings and rings—but the few standard items remain popular with all the women who can afford gold. Of course, ideas such as those attached to the silver fashioned by Gab Gab in terms of its curative properties and as a charm against misfortune have been lost. The shiny new gold is prized as a symbol of modernity and fashion but its protective powers remain vague and undefined.

Allegiance to the old ways, however, is still present in the oasis. Some women declare they have no interest in gold and prefer to go without, or to wear plain, modern silver bangles rather than turn to cheaper gold-dipped jewelry that is available in the city souqs. Some of the elderly have resisted the lure of modern jewelry altogether, and continue to wear daily the traditional silver or metal hoop earrings and *dimjung* bangles, although the bird and fish patterns that adorn the bangles have almost worn away through daily tasks and rubbing against their clothes. "We old ones don't understand the gold," they say. Many keep a few bits and pieces of silver jewelry in a tin, as a keepsake from the ensemble with which they were once festooned on ceremonial occasions. Certain pieces, such as the triangular *tilaksit* pendants and the small jeweled *gingilts*, have been retained to enrich and add ancestral luster to the surfaces of ceremonial dresses and headshawls. These items are imbued with cherished memories and suggest stories they can tell their grandchildren. They also act as a record of the past that will be invaluable when interest in the past becomes more important in the oasis.

Siwans have modified many of the changes that have affected them in the last decades to conform to their tastes and culture, but this has not always been the case. The advent of gold, for example, has visibly changed some traditional behavior. For example, in the past when silver was essential to festive costume and ceremony, it was common for the less well off to borrow jewelry for weddings and the *eids* from their richer relations and neighbors. Everybody who wanted to be was thus similarly adorned, and felt themselves part of the group. Gold jewelry, on the other hand, is not shared in this way, but serves rather to emphasize divisions in wealth within the community.

Wearing the black face-veil in addition to the Siwan shawl, the *tarfutet*, when a woman is outside the home, has tended to erode the shawl's traditional importance. Indeed, on a visit to the oasis a few years ago I found that when the women traveled outside the oasis they were increasingly wearing a cloak they pulled over their heads in place of the *tarfutet*. Made up in dark green, blue, brown, or beige, or black for older women, it enables them to blend more easily into the outside world and to feel less conspicuous. Now, some young women say they believe the *tarfutet*, although it has always been a precious symbol of Siwan society, may one day be replaced by the ubiquitous all-enveloping *milaya*. On the other hand, there are Siwans who say that the *tarfutet* is so deeply entrenched in their culture that it will always be worn in the oasis. I only hope they are right. It is quite clear that this traditional shawl is a symbol of Siwa's heritage going back hundreds of years. To lose it in the interest of uniformity would be, to my mind, a catastrophe.

In spite of the adaptations to Siwan traditions and the optimistic attempts at revival, there is a concern among some in the oasis that the rush for modernity has been too rapid and that customs of the past have been discounted too easily. Traditional embroidered clothes and artifacts have disappeared from the oasis as families have taken advantage of the demand from tourists to sell them. There is concern that a great deal of Siwa's silver jewelry has been sold to merchants or removed by collectors. Pieces made by Master Gab Gab are now more likely to be found exhibited, or stored away, in foreign museums and private collections than seen in Siwa. Indeed, apart from the pieces displayed in the Siwa House Museum, or owned by a few wealthy families, there is hardly any jewelry made by Master Gab Gab left in the oasis. Lamenting the disappearance, a young Siwan businessman told me that he hopes one day to buy back an *adrim* and *aghraw* made by Gab Gab and display them on a wall of his house.

On the other hand, the demand for Siwan jewelry and textiles from outside, and the support of the local SCDEC Siwa Community Development and Environmental Conservation Association, has had the effect of stimulating the revival of these traditional handicrafts and restoring the link with the past. The Egypt Crafts Centre/Fair Trade, and the Italian COSPE Egypt arranged for a small group of Siwan men, including the young artist Yousef Ibrahim Eissa, to have a few months, training in the art of the silversmith in the silver workshops of Khan al-Khalili in Cairo, followed by a period of training in Siwa. I was in Siwa when their first rings were returned to them having been assessed and then hallmarked by the Assay Office in Cairo. Siwans showed a great deal of interest in this project and, when I was in the oasis a few years later, the young men were beginning to make a range of jewelry, including smaller, wearable, and affordable items, such as rings, using Gab Gab's pieces as their lodestar. They were also developing their own original designs depicting the natural scenery of the oasis. This initiative was, it is true, designed to satisfy the tourist trade, but it was also expected to appeal to local people, and restore their interest in silver jewelry. It was their hope that some Siwan women would wear their jewelry and that in a small way the long and important tradition of wearing silver pieces made by local silversmiths would be revived. However, this project has been slow to get off the ground despite the young men's enthusiasm. A silversmith requires at least five years, training, and because there were no established silversmiths remaining in the oasis this has not been possible.

A more recent project has been the training of three girls to work as silversmiths. One of the young women told me, "At first silversmithing was for men because it was thought to be too dangerous for women. When we were eventually allowed to do the training we were chosen for our artistic ability, such as if we could paint." Since completing an extra, brief course at a Faculty of Arts Education in Cairo, provided by the EU-funded Euromed Heritage programme, she was equipped to teach other young people. This talented young woman now manages the metalsmithing workshop in a modern training center in Siwa where she teaches girls the art of the silversmith. In her own workshop at home, she showed me many of her earrings and bangles, including innovative silver earrings decorated with a fragment of silk embroidered with a Siwan motif. As well as producing jewelry to sell to tourists she is delighted to have some Siwan customers. A particularly successful project has been to make a silver ornament to place in the center of the *suweidi* necklace. She and her two colleagues sell their silver and more affordable copper jewelry to visitors to the training center and from the shops around the town. Like the male silversmiths, the women generally prefer to use and adapt Gab Gab's designs, which are suffused with cultural meaning and which they greatly admire. This also pleases visitors who have heard about his work and expect to see 'Siwan' jewelry in the shops around the town. These young female silversmiths have, of course, one advantage over the men, which is their direct contact with the women who become their customers.

Sometimes in Siwa I meet a friend who is wearing very attractive earrings or a ring they say was made by Siwan Mr. Abdallah Baghi. Mr. Baghi learned to make silver pieces in the oasis from a jeweler from the Delta, and was instrumental in introducing the training program for jewelry for the young men and in encouraging women silversmiths. He is director of education for the Siwa District. He also opened the first handicraft shop in the town in 1987. He is knowledgeable about Gab Gab's jewelry and has a fine collection of pieces made by him.

Embroidery also has been revitalized by tourism, and by supplying markets outside the oasis. Many Siwan women send embroidery and baskets, by way of their children, to be sold in the handicraft shops. A few sell to women tourists from home. For many years there have been women who embroider textiles for shops and hotel boutiques in Cairo. For instance, a Siwan friend—the wife of a man with a handicraft business—produced excellent embroidered garments: textiles with embroidered patterns made to order; and baskets to send to Cairo or to shops in the Siwa souq, made by herself and a group of carefully selected women. She provided the materials, like mother-of-pearl buttons and silk thread, both for embroidery and to decorate the baskets, and rope for the baskets. She told me she might buy a basket from its maker for 100 Egyptian pounds, which would retail in the shops for 150 Egyptian pounds, of which the shopkeeper would take 15 Egyptian pounds. She, who had bought the silks and buttons, and paid the rope-maker 10 Egyptian pounds, would receive the remainder. Another woman friend called Naama sold handicrafts made by neighbors and relatives to women tourists from her home. Her children would bring the tourists to her. A neighbour told me that they could speak some English, and I saw that the young girl in the family, whose drawing of the *asherah nauak* dress is shown in figure 91, was cognizant with the handicrafts.

In Siwa today, there are young women who are starting similar businesses, doing embroidery of a high standard—often producing their own innovative designs and now sourcing their materials in the oasis. In Aghurmi I met zamzam, who provides the manager of a shop in the Shali souk with textiles of the quality he appreciates. As we chatted about her work, she was stitching the outline of the design on a collar, with the tiniest red backstitches, for a friend's trousseau. Later, in the souq, I was delighted to see some of her work being appreciated and sold. And this was despite the fact that it was relatively expensive and that few of the shops were open due to the scarcity of tourists through Egypt's political transition. It was also in the summer, when the numbers of tourists always drop.

Writing of one such enterprise, Ilaria Bilancetti, who worked with Siwan handicrafts as consultant for the COSPE Siwa–Tangier project, says that the young woman who is the organizer—taking orders from four local shops—prefers to work on "new embroidered items directed to the tourist market instead of embroidered items for the bride's trousseaux . . . . Moreover, working for the bazaars provides a quicker payment, while traditional garments take months to be finished as well as to be paid for."[93] Tourism has also inspired the development of new projects and facilities for weaving. Girls produce hand-woven kilims and tufted rugs and tapestries similar to ones made in Kerdassa.

Amid the local, Egyptian and, foreign initiatives concerned with handicrafts, one large well-established, and successful enterprise, set up by Leila Neamatalla, employs talented Siwan girls to embroider for a global haute-couture market. Traditional Siwan designs are adapted and new patterns created to suit modern tastes. The girls work in an attractive atelier and the women at home. As well as embroidering clothes, they decorate accessories like bags, shoes, and leather-decorated silver jewelry. These pieces are of such high quality that they have been seen on the catwalks of Italy. It is encouraging to see girls and women gain respect for their exquisite work. A girl's income and needlework skills will enable her to gather an ample trousseau and improve her opportunities for marriage. Though she is enthusiastic about the clothes she makes, she is unlikely to include them in her trousseau because they do not fit the Siwa aesthetic.

This does not mean that modern designs were introduced to the traditional code of embroidery without encountering any difficulties. For example, Ilaria Bilancetti says that though it may be easy for a woman to reproduce a particular pattern, difficulties may arise when the designer wants them to adopt a more original approach. She says that Ellen Raven, a Danish designer who has been working with Siwan embroiderers for five years, explained to her that even the use of different colors can be confusing: "Whenever I introduce new colors I have to explain to them the correspondence with the traditional ones in order to make them understand how to use them. I never use more than five colors at a time and then I have to tell them which one has to be used like the green, which one like the red and so on."[94] Research into the field of color shows that color perception and judgements vary across cultures. However, when Siwan women do their own work they use new, vivid colors, it seems, quite freely.

Older Siwan women, who are experts in the traditional embroidery that may have been practiced in the oasis for hundreds of years, sometimes resent the intrusion of new designs, colors, and techniques to their highly valued craft. The rich symbolism of the embroidered clothes still speaks to them and the 'new embroidery,' which reconfigures the symbolic order, inhibits their desire to maintain a distinct identity.

The women's evolving embroidered and woven patterns mirror the changes taking place in their lifestyle, such as more girls completing high school before they marry, some girls saying they will marry later, and some not at all—although they are still expected to marry by the age of eighteen. There are now a few Siwan girls teaching in the oasis and more in Marsa Matrouh—thanks to special facilities that were arranged for their training, as girls may not leave the oasis to attend college. Some women and girls now go to the mosque, especially in Ramadan, Eid al-Fitr, and Eid al-Adha. Commenting on a radical recent innovation for girls to wear a *niqab* and a black *milaya* over their Egyptian clothes, which they apparently find empowering and another step toward emancipation, a girl said to me, "With the internet and the *niqab* our lives will change forever!"

Glossary

(A/S): Both Siwi and Arabic

Siwan Words

abernaas: baby's bonnet

abesha: discontinued practice in which the groom gives the bride's mother money in recognition of the bride's virginity

adrim: engraved silver disc

agabez: cowrie shell

agnin: storage basket

ahgraw: silver torque

ajrang: clay jar

akbir: the Siwan man's *gallabiya*

akbir il harir: the Siwan bride's traditional striped silk wedding dress

akbir nwasa: the standard wide Siwan dress

akodah: basket measure

arabu: basket measure

arak n' tishka: ceremony of washing the bride's feet, traditionally on the third day of the wedding

aras negbesen: necklace of cowrie shells, coral, and glass beads

arus: wedding

asafah: marriage contract

asenhab: ritual scattering of wedding gifts

asherah hawak azdaf: the traditional black embroidered wedding dress

asherah nauak: the Siwan white embroidered wedding dress

astin: a needle-shaped tool used in basket making

atba: seal

ateelun: date gardens

atras: ceremony in which the bride's hair is styled

atrash naman: bride bathing ceremony

atuk: cotton embroidered collar

azume: machine embroidery

barsh: marriage mat

boab: town crier

careta: small wooden carriage

carusa: donkey cart

cushit: shoulder-length, plaited hairstyle with a fringe

dahwera: snack eaten between 10:00 and 11:00 a.m.

defira: hairstyle with two plaits

deket: tasseled belt

diblitsh: wide bangle

dimjun: bangles worn on each wrist by married women

dishish: dish of crushed wheat, tomatoes, onions, and offal that marks the end of a wedding

dulula: garden sun shelter

emendal: black silk shawl

emensi: pans

emjir: pruning knife used in the date gardens

gulah: female ghost

gumar: white heart of the date palm

gutan: plaited silk ropes to attach to the bodice of the embroidered wedding dress

gutra: Arab man's headress

idhar: palm sling for climbing trees

igawi: incense burned to ward off the evil eye

iharuzang: checkered pattern

ilazim: necklace of amber, silver, and, sometimes, coral beads

inhuli: jewelry chest

is-sudan: hoop earrings

itgarfet enishti: 'winter room' used in cold weather

itha: time of day, around 11:00 a.m.

izeat: donkey

jird (A/S): long white sheet of wool or silk that was worn by rich Siwan men and Bedouin

jowee: unguent used during the *seboua* ceremony

jubit (in Arabic *jubba*): thick woolen tunic

kersheef (A/S): mud containing salt collected from the shores of the salt lakes

khamsa wa khamesa: Siwan embroidery motif representing two hands, that is, five and five fingers together

klact: clay used in building

lagbi: drink made from the sap of the date palm

libsees: dessert of crushed dates served at christenings and weddings

ligsas: silver and amber bridal ornament

litshinab nagil il harir: striped patch, typically stitched into side seams at the hem of the Siwan *akbir nwasa* dress

lugyeet: head ornament of red leather, mother-of-pearl buttons, and metal hoops

maarbua: visitors' room for men only

mahbis: ring

mahzen: foodstuffs

makalay: clay cup

makhmakh: broth made of the leaves of the purslane plant

margunah: basket

menina: cookies made with oil, served at weddings and other celebrations

meruid: brass or silver wand for applying henna

nakbir il harir: hand-woven striped wedding shawl

natiyac: 'narrow dress' worn under the wide *akbir nwasa* dress

ogeed: man

rumi: sturdy, loose-woven cotton material

saa: basket measure

sad: earring

salhayat: necklace of crescent-shaped pendants and coral and silver beads

sebait tarust: second day of the wedding

shemata: seventh day of the wedding

shemata natnu: one week after the seventh day of the wedding

sinit: scent, perfume

sirwal: baggy trousers, narrow from knee to ankle

srawelin khatem: Siwan white cotton embroidered trousers

stahnamas: wide hallway of Siwan homes

suar: heavy bangle

suweidi: necklace of coral, onyx, and silver

taarfet narus: bridal room

tabint: mud bread oven

tad: finger

tadelt: basket for dates and olives

tadlilt: red leather bridal headdress

taglentenu: dates cooked with flour, oil, and water

takadumt: midwife

takatusht: palm branch

taksart achtar: type of embroidery

tangkult: red leather kohl pot

tankutat (nhilba): a dry bread made with fenugreek (and eaten hot with water, sugar, and butter)

tarfutet: traditional blue-and-white checked shawl

tarust: bride

tasalt: kohl

tashabat: large silver amulet case

taziri: crescent moon

tchukabuk: chattering

tcoset: plaited hairstyle using thirty-three braids, traditionally worn by married women

tde akbir lihrir: smarter and more colorful version of the *tde rumi akbir nwasa*

tde rumi akbir nwasa: everyday blue striped dress

tederbolain: simple plaited hairstyle

teenee: dates (fruit)

teezignit: needle

telaia: unsymmetrical

teltee: woman

tignikt nashral: crochet

tilakeen: crescent head decoration worn by a bride

tilaksit: triangular cast openwork pendent

tim shamart al-tarust: incense burner for a bride

timisnakt: green and red beaded necklet hung with chains and plates

tiquat: tools

tirkirt: hairstyle worn by women until the 1950s

tiset: round, flat, palm-leaf tray to serve visitors chick peas, peanuts, and sweets.

tobahejt: symmetrical

tora: game played with stones

troket: traditional black embroidered headshawl

tulintfukt: 'eye of the sun,' a name given to mother-of-pearl buttons

twetwat: shining

wagaba: local time system for watering of the date gardens

yizme: to sew

zaggal (pl. *zaggala*): male laboror or farm worker

zir: water jar

zrabin: shoes

Arabic Words

abaya: woman's cloak

ahdad: blacksmith

arous/arousa: bridegroom/bride

asha: (light) evening meal

asriya: light snack eaten around 5:00 p.m.

attar: seller of herbs, homeopathic medicines, beads, etc., who may travel
  or have a shop in a souq

ayn (in Siwi *tot*): eye or spring of water

berseem: clover

dahab: gold

darawish: members of a religious community

djinn: demon or genie; vengeful spirit, or (less often) one that is helpful to
  humans; frequently mentioned in the Qur'an

eid: local or religious festival or feast

fada: silver

fellah: peasant farmer

fikh: magician, also supplies clients with amulets

fitur: breakfast

fuul: stewed dried fava beans

ghada: lunch; main meal of the day, usually served around 1:00 p.m.

harir: silk

hilal: crescent moon

hilba: fenugreek

humusiya: chickpea; necklace of round gold beads

gallabiya: classic Egyptian full-length robe, worn by men and women

karkadeh: a drink made from hibiscus flowers

khamsa: the number five; also a name for the Hand of Fatima symbol (a
  hand with five fingers and often an eye in the center)

khatem: seal; a decorative device
kirdan: elaborate gold necklace
kohl: eye-liner
leilat al-dukhla: 'night of entering,' the wedding night
leilat al-henna: 'night of the henna' when the bride's hands, legs, and feet are decorated with henna by skilled henna artists from the community
(alf) mabrouk: congratulations
mahr: marriage payment
milaya: wrap worn by women throughout the Middle East
moda: fashion
moulid: festival of a saint
mulukhiya: soup made from leaves of the Jew's mallow plant
niqab: face covering that leaves only the eyes visible
qabila: tribe
qirsh: Egyptian piaster
rumi: a loosely woven cotton (or linen) material
sadaf: shell, mother-of-pearl
seboua: ceremony that takes place seven days after a birth
senduq: (marriage) chest
shakshouka: vegetable and egg ragout
shal: headshawl
sheikh: honorific title given to a religious or civil leader of a group; chief of a tribe respected for wisdom and courage; sometimes used interchangeably with *fikh*.
sirwal: baggy pants, very wide at the waist and fitted tightly around the lower leg
suhour: breakfast eaten during Ramadan before fasting begins
tabliya: low table
tarha: veil
tatris: embroidery
zaffa: wedding procession
zaghareet: undulating cries of joy
zakat: a religious tax for the benefit of the poor; one of the five pillars of Islam
zaraar: button
zaytouna: olive; necklace of rhomboid-shaped gold beads
zikr: religious, trance-like dance

Motifs and Meanings

bird: messenger between earth and heaven.

bulla: lens-shaped (originally Etruscan) amulet worn by Roman children hanging from a necklace.

coins: given away for good luck.

crescent: often depicted with a star, signifying paradise. It conveys an emblematic meaning throughout the Islamic world, but predates Islam as an emblem: in ancient times it was symbolic of fertility. Roman men and women are believed to have worn it against the evil eye and it retains vestiges of these beliefs today.

cowrie shell: used to protect against the evil eye and to promote fertility.

eye: an image of the eye or an abstract representation of the eye is seen as the most effective way to counteract the evil eye.

eyebrow: depicted as a curved line, or the curves joined to make a pattern. A protection against the evil eye.

fish: represents water, rain, and the fertility of the earth.

flowers and leaves: symbolize a beautiful landscape and fertility.

five: *khamsa* in Arabic, possesses a magical value against the evil eye, as do symbols such as the hand that have five elements to them.

hand: since ancient times a symbol of strength, power, and protection.

heart: in Islam relates to contemplation and spiritual life rather than to emotions. Heart amulets date back to ancient Egypt where they took the form of a vase and were made in various materials including glass. In Coptic Egypt it was embroidered on woven textiles.

henna: associated with purity and protection.

horseshoe: a protection against the evil eye; related to the crescent.

palm tree: tree of life; associated with fertility.

salt: purifies and cleanses, and used against the evil eye.

shell: associated with fertility.

snake: in Berber arts often represented by a wavy line or zigzag; associated with the phallus, the libido, and fertility.

sun: represented by motifs such as a sunflower, rosette, ring, and cross or dot within a circle. In Siwa a mother-of-pearl button is called 'eye of the sun' *(tutinyfukt)*, and is thought to be a symbol of creative energy.

sun, moon, crescent moon, and star: symbolize fecundity, and are believed to be prophylactic.

sweets: Giving people sweets "at joyful events or after particular successes" is thought by Spooner to be "an effort to prevent envy."[95]

water: symbol of purification and fertility, depicted with a wavy line.

Notes

1   Marianne Ellis, *Embroideries and Samplers from Islamic Egypt* (Oxford, UK: Ashmolean Museum, 2001), 49.

2   C. Spring and J. Hudson, *Silk in Africa* (London: British Museum Press, 2002), 10–11.

3   Anne-Marie Bouttiaux, *African Costumes and Textiles from the Berbers to the Zulus: The Zaire and Marcel Mis Collection* (Milan: 5 Continents Editions, 2008).

4   Ahmed Fakhry, *The Oases of Egypt, Volume One: Siwa Oasis* (Cairo: The American University in Cairo Press, 1973), 94.

5   Fakhry, *Oases of Egypt*, 93.

6   F. Cailliaud, *Voyage á Méroe – a Syouah et dans cinc autres Oasis, fait dans les années 1819, 1820, et 1822* (Paris: Imprimerie Royale, 1826), vol. 1, 95.

7   G. Rohlfs, *Three Months in the Libyan Desert* (Cairo: The American University in Cairo Press, 2005).

8   Fathi Malim, *Oasis: Siwa from the Inside: Traditions, Customs and Magic* (Egypt: Al Katan, 2001), 69.

9   C.D. Belgrave, *Siwa: The Oasis of Jupiter Ammon* (London: John Lane The Bodley Head, 1923), 137.

10 At the time of writing, 1 US dollar is roughly equivalent to 7 Egyptian pounds (or 700 Egyptian piasters).

11 Abd El-Aziz Abd El-Rahman Aldumairy, *Siwa: Past and Present* (Alexandria: Yasso, 2005), 5.

12 One feddan is roughly equal to one acre.

13   Walter Cline, "Notes on the People of Siwah and El Garah in the Libyan Desert," *General Series in Anthropology*, Harvard, no. 4, (Menasha, WI: George Banta Publishing Company, 1936), 38. Walter Cline was in Siwa from December 1926 to February 1927.

14   Cline, "Notes," 36.

15   Cline, "Notes," 36.

16   Aldumairy, *Siwa*, 51. Aldumairy says, "The crevice is so tiny that the workers must send a small boy into the interior to collect the material."

17   O. Bates, "Siwan Pottery," *Harvard African Studies*, vol. 11 (Cambridge, MA: Harvard University Press, 1918), 299–304.

18   Fakhry, *Oases of Egypt*, 22.

19   L.L. Giddy, *Egyptian Oases: Bahariya, Dakhla, Farafra and Kharga during Pharaonic Times* (Warminster UK: Aris and Philips, 1986), see chapter entitled "Routes from Siwa." Also discussed in Cassandra Vivian, *The Western Desert of Egypt: An Explorer's Handbook* (Cairo: The American University in Cairo Press, 2000); Fakhry, *Oases of Egypt*; and Cailliaud, *Voyage*.

20   Frederick Horneman, *The Journal of Horneman's Travels from Cairo to Mourzouk: The Capital of Fezzan in Africa in the Years 1797–8* (London: W. Bulmer and Co., 1802), 11.

21   Cailliaud, *Voyage*, vol. 2, 11.

22   G.E. Simpson, *The Heart of Libya: The Siwa Oasis, Its People, Customs and Sport* (London: H.F. and G. Witherby, 1929), 119.

23   G. Steindorf, *Durch die Lybysche Wüste zur Amonsoase* (Bielfeld and Leipzig: Velhagen and Klasing, 1904), 113

24   Belgrave, *Siwa*, 140.

25   Belgrave, *Siwa*, 141.

26   Belgrave, *Siwa*, 141.

27   Belgrave, *Siwa*, 140.

28   H.V. Morton, *Through the Lands of the Bible* (London: Methuen, 1938), 190–91.

29   Belgrave, *Siwa*, 134.

30   Belgrave, *Siwa*, 133–35.

31   Malim, *Oasis*, 34.

32   Muhammad Ibrahim Moussa, writing about Siwan culture and food on the website *http://www.siwaoasis.com/siwa_food.html*.

33   Malim, *Oasis*, 30.

34   Aldumairy, *Siwa*, 33.

35   Belgrave, *Siwa*, 253.

36   Fakhry, *Oases of Egypt*, 61–62.

37   Claude Savary, *Egypte, oasis d'Amun-Siwa: Musée d'ethnographie, Genève, 1986* (Geneva: le Musée d'ethnographie, [c1986]), 39 and 41.

38   C. Fabius, *Mehndi: The Art of Henna Painting* (New York: Three Rivers Press, 1998), 17.

39   Cline, "Notes," 45.

40   A. Fisher, *Africa Adorned* (London: Collins, 1984), 194.

41   Malim, *Oasis*, 128.

42   Malim, *Oasis*, 112.

43   Belgrave, *Siwa*, 230–31.

44   Aldumairy, *Siwa*, 31.

45   Belgrave, *Siwa*, 216.

46   Cline, "Notes," 46.

47   Savary, *Egypte*, 47; Malim, *Oasis*, 58.

48   Cline, "Notes," 47.

49   Cline, "Notes," 47.

50   Fakhry, *Oases of Egypt*, 57.

51   E.W. Lane, *An Account of the Manners and Customs of the Modern Egyptians* (London: Ward, Locke and Co, 1871), vol. 1, 217.

52   Aldumairy, *Siwa*, 50–51. Aldumairy says if indeed the Spring of the Sun (Cleopatra's Spring) "did exist already during the fifth century BC, because of its clarity, size and location near the Ammonian complex, it undoubtedly would have had special significance in ancient times."

53   Horneman, *Journal*, 17.

54   Belgrave, *Siwa*, 212–13.

55   Cline, "Notes," 44.

56   Moussa, writing about Siwan culture and circumcision, *http://www.siwaoasis.com/siwa_circumcision.html.*

57   Belgrave, *Siwa*, 235–36.

58   Similar precautions have been taken by peoples in other regions of the world, notably in Indonesia.

59   R. Sieber and F. Herreman, eds., *Hair in African Art and Culture* (New York: Prestel, 2000), 153. This widowhood practice may have entered the oasis through the influence of West African slaves who remained there and whose observances were drawn on. For example, among the Yoruba of Nigeria "a widow was required to undo her braids, leave her hair dishevelled, and remain indoors until the completion of her husband's funeral rites, which may last about three months." See also M.M. Abdallah, "Siwan Customs," *Harvard African Studies* (Cambridge, MA: Harvard University Press, 1917), vol. 1, 58; Cline, "Notes," 51.

60   Horneman, *Journal*, 17. Horneman probably mistook the star decoration for flowers. Gertrude Elizabeth Simpson, who visited Siwa, repeats Horneman's description, but the photograph in her book shows that the *adrim* was engraved with the cross and stars design (*Heart*, 184).

61   K.R. Brown, "If Only the Dead Could Talk: An Update on the East German and Hunnish Jewelry Collection at the Metropolitan Museum of Art," in Adriana Calinescu, ed., *Ancient Jewelry and Archaeology* (Bloomington, IN: Indiana University Press, 1996), 230–31. The form of the

Siwan torque resembles a type of round tapering Germanic (East German) fifth-century torque. The hook and eye closure is made by folding back and wrapping the wire on both sides, or only the eye. See David Crystal, ed., *The Penguin Encyclopedia* (London: Penguin Books, 2002), 1398.

62   J.F. Jereb, *Arts and Crafts of Morocco* (London: Thames and Hudson, 1995).

63   P.W. Schienerl, "Female Jewelry from Siwa Oasis," in *Acta Ethnographica Academiae Scientiarum Hungaricae* 29 (Budapest: Akademiai Kiado, 1980), 167–80.

64   Susan Weeks, "The Costume and Ornaments of the West Desert Bedouin," in *Cairo Today* 6, no. 9 (September 1985).

65   Frank Bliss and Marlis Weissenberger, "Jewelry from the Siwa Oasis," *Ornament* 6, no. 4 (1983), 6–11.

66   H. Camps-Fabrer, *Bijoux Berbères d'Algérie* (Aix-en-Provence: Edisud, 1990), 89–91; British Museum, *Jewelry through 7000 Years* (London: British Museum Press, 1976), 168.

67   *Timisnakt* pendants were donated to the British Museum in 1920 by W. Seymour Walker, who wrote the book *The Siwi Language*, first published in London in 1921.

68   Savary, (*Egypte*, 62),describes a necklace called *uwar uwar* that was worn by the Siwan women as "a double stranded necklace made of very small beads which look like gold." I have not seen this piece in Siwa today, but in the 1950s I often saw similar necklaces of gold glass beads from India in the jewelry souq in Riyadh, Saudi Arabia. I believe they were used to promote fertility.

69   Looking to the ancient world, red coral with jet was a favorite combination used by the Romans.

70   Simpson, *Heart*, 184. Gertrude Simpson joined a small tourist expedition that crossed the desert to Siwa in cars. The trip was organized by Captain Hillier of the Libyan Oases Association. Hillier's rest house and hotel were comfortably furnished with Bedouin rugs and easy chairs, and provided every luxury "even to the cocktail" (*Heart*, 105–106). The women in the group were invited to meet Siwan women. She describes their hairstyle and hair decoration in her book.

71   D. Haldane, *Islamic Bookbindings in the Victoria and Albert Museum* (London: World of Islam Festival Trust, 1983), 21. The Star of David is an ancient motif that has come to symbolize Jewry, but it has appeared in many cultures. It was employed in Islam, for example in tooled designs for Islamic bookbindings in the fourteenth and fifteenth centuries.

72   Horneman, *Journal*, 17.

73   Ahmed Fakhry, *Bahariyah and Farafra* with a new introduction by Anthony J. Mills (Cairo: The American University in Cairo Press, 2003), 42.

74   Bliss and Weissenberger, "Jewelry," 6–11.

75   A. Fakhry, *Oases of Egypt*, 55, f.n. 3.

76   Azza Fahmy, "Peasant and Sha'bi Jewelry," in *Enchanted Jewelry of Egypt: The Traditional Art and Craft* (Cairo: The American University in Cairo Press, 2007), 25–53.

77   Belgrave, *Siwa*, 148.

78   Andrea B. Rugh, *Reveal and Conceal: Dress in Contemporary Egypt* (Cairo: The American University in Cairo Press, 1987), 12.

79   J. Balfour-Paul, *Indigo in the Arab World* (Abingdon, UK: Routledge, 1997), 82.

80   C. J. Becker, *Amazigh Arts in Morocco: Women Shaping Berber Identity* (Austin: University of Texas Press, 2006), 68.

81   Malim, *Oasis*, 9.

82   Belgrave, *Siwa*, 148.

83   C. Spring and J. Hudson, *North African Textiles* (London: British Museum Press, 1995), 53; M. Sijelmassi, *Les Arts Traditionnels au Maroc* (Paris: Art Creation Realisation Edition, 1986), 35.

84   Marianne Ellis in a discussion at the Victoria and Albert Museum in 2006 identified for me the stitches used on a Siwan wedding dress and leather shoes.

85   Ellis, discussion at the V & A, 2006.

86   See Rugh, *Reveal*, 54; D. Ammoun, *Crafts of Egypt* (Cairo: The American University in Cairo Press, 1991); Spring and Hudson, *North African Textiles*, 5.

87   Spring and Hudson, *North African Textiles*, 113. The authors say this is due to "the relative proximity of Cairo to the east, and the consequently greater availability of dyed yarns, or, perhaps by the influence of Siwa to the west, with its own colorful and highly individual tradition of embroidery." Fakhry points out that "at least one village in Bahariyah is predominantly populated by people of Siwan origin." (*Bahariyah and Farafra*, 21).

88   Vivian, *Western Desert*, 123.

89   Malim, *Oasis*, 54.

90   Malim, *Oasis*, 48.

91   S. Weir, *Palestinian Costume* (London: British Museum Press, 1989), 269.

92   Spring and Hudson, *North African Textiles*, 69. The authors describe how during a special ceremony on the evening of her wedding day the splendidly attired "Tlemcen (Algeria) bride is presented formally to the assembled guests" and "stands motionless, with her arms at her sides and her eyes closed. It has been suggested that this posture may be designed to protect the resplendent bride from malevolent glances."

93   I. Bilancetti, *Searching for Siwan Embroidery* (Florence: Cooperazione per lo Sviluppo dei Paesi Emergents (COSPE), 2012), 40.

94   Bilancetti, *Searching for Embroidery*, 40.

95   B. Spooner, "The Evil Eye in the Middle East," in C. Malony, ed., *The Evil Eye* (New York: Columbia University Press, 1976), 81.

Bibliography

Abdallah, M.M. "Siwan Customs." *Harvard African Studies* 1. Cambridge, MA: Harvard University Press, 1917.

Abu-Lughod, L. *Veiled Sentiments: Honour and Poetry in a Bedouin Society.* Berkeley, CA: University of California Press, 1986.

Aldumairy, Abd El-Aziz Abd-El Rahman. *Siwa: Past and Present.* Alexandria: Yasso, 2005.

Ammar, H. *Growing up in an Egyptian Village: Silwa, Province of Aswan.* London: Routledge & Paul, 1954.

Ammoun, D. *Crafts of Egypt.* Cairo: The American University in Cairo Press, 1991.

Baali, F. "Ibn Kaldoun." In *The Oxford Encyclopedia of the Modern Islamic World.* Vol. 2. Oxford, UK: Oxford University Press, 1995. p. 164.

Bachinger, R., and P.W. Schienerl. *Silberschmuck aus Ägypten.* Frankfurt: Galerie Exler, 1984.

Balfour-Paul, J. *Indigo in the Arab World.* Abingdon, UK: Routledge, 1997.

Bates, O. "Siwan Pottery." *Harvard African Studies* 11. Cambridge, MA: Harvard University Press, 1918. pp. 299–304

Becker, C.J. *Amazigh Arts in Morocco: Women Shaping Berber Identity.* Austin, TX: University of Texas Press, 2006.

Belgrave, C.D. *Siwa: the Oasis of Jupiter Ammon.* London: John Lane The Bodley Head, 1923.

Bilancetti, Ilaria. *Searching for Siwan Embroidery.* Florence: Cooperazione per lo Sviluppo dei Paesi Emergents (COSPE), 2012.

Bliss, Frank and Marlis Weissenberger. "Jewelry from the Siwa Oasis." *Ornament* 6, no. 4 (1983): 6–11.

Boardman, John. "The Archaeology of Jewelry." In *Ancient Jewelry and Archaeology*, edited by Adriana Calinescu. Bloomington, IN: Indiana University Press, 1996. pp. 3–13.

Bouttiaux, Anne-Marie. *African Costumes and Textiles: From the Berbers to the Zulus: The Zaire and Marcel Mis Collection*. Milan: 5 Continents, 2008.

Bowie, Fiona. *The Anthropology of Religion: An Introduction*. Oxford, UK: Blackwell, 2006.

Braudel, F. *The Mediterranean in the Ancient World*. London: Penguin, 2001.

Brett, M., and E. Fentress. *The Berbers*. Oxford, UK: Blackwell, 1997.

British Museum. *Jewelry through 7000 Years*. London: British Museum Press, 1976.

Brown, K. Reynolds. "If Only the Dead Could Talk: An Update on the East German and Hunnish Jewelry Collection at the Metropolitan Museum of Art." In *Ancient Jewelry and Archaeology*, edited by Adriana Calinescu. Bloomington, IN: Indiana University Press, 1996. pp. 224–35.

Cailliaud, F. *Voyage á Méroe … a Syouah et dans cinq autres oasis, fait dans les années 1819, 1820 et 1822*, 4 vols. Paris: Imprimerie Royale, 1826.

Calinescu, A., ed. *Ancient Jewelry and Archaeology*. Bloomington, IN: Indiana University Press, 1996.

Camps-Febrer, H. *Bijoux Berbères d'Algérie*. Aix-en-Provence: Edisud, 1990.

Carroll, D. Lee. *Looms and Textiles of the Copts: First Millennium Egyptian Textiles in the Carl Austin Rietz Collection of the California Academy of Sciences*. Seattle, WA: California Academy of Sciences, 1989.

Cline, W. "Notes on the People of Siwah and El Garah in the Libyan Desert." *General Series in Anthropology*, Harvard no. 4. Menasha, WI: George Banta Publishing Company, 1936.

Crystal, D., ed. *The Penguin Encyclopedia*. London: Penguin Books, 2002.

Diamante, J. *Silver Speaks: The Traditional Jewelry of the Middle East*. Washington, DC: The Bead Society, 2002.

Doumato, E.A. "Marriage and Divorce: Modern Practice." In *The Oxford Encyclopedia of the Modern Islamic World*. Vol. 3. Oxford, UK: Oxford University Press, 1995, pp. 50–54.

Dubin, S.D. *The History of Beads: from 30,000 B.C. to the Present*. London: Thames and Hudson, 1987.

Ellis, Marianne. *Embroideries and Samplers from Islamic Egypt*. Oxford, UK: Ashmolean Museum, 2001.

Elworthy, F.T. *The Evil Eye: The Origins and Practices of Superstition*. London: Collier-Maxmillan, 1970.

Fabius, C. *Mehndi: The Art of Henna Painting*. New York: Three Rivers Press, 1998.

Fage, J.D. *A History of Africa*. 2nd ed. London: Routledge, 1988.

Fahmy, Azza. *Enchanted Jewelry of Egypt: The Traditional Art and Craft*. Cairo: The American University in Cairo Press, 2007.

Fakhry, A. *Bahariyah and Farafra* with a new introduction by Anthony J. Mills. Cairo: The American University in Cairo Press, 2003.

———. *The Oases of Egypt, Volume 1: Siwa Oasis*. Cairo: The American University in Cairo Press, 1973.

Fisher, A. *Africa Adorned*. London: Collins, 1984.

Francis, Peter. *Beads of the World*. Atglen, PA: Schiffer Publishing, 1994.

Ghannam, F. *Space, Relocation, and the Politics of Identity in a Global Cairo*. Berkeley, CA: University of California Press, 2002.

Ghosh, A. *The Imam and the Indian*. Delhi: Ravi Dayal, 2002.

Giddy, L.L. *Egyptian Oases: Bahariya, Dakhla, Farafra and Kharga during Pharaonic Times*. Warminster, UK: Aris and Philips, 1986.

Gillow, John. *Color and Creativity across a Continent*. London: Thames and Hudson, 2003.

Haldane, D. *Islamic Bookbindings in the Victoria and Albert Museum*. London: The World of Islam Festival Trust, 1983.

Hall, Rosalind. *Egyptian Textiles*. Princes Riseborough, UK: Shire Publications, 2001.

Harris, J. *5000 Years of Textiles*. London: British Museum Press, in association with The Whitworth Art Gallery and The Victoria and Albert Museum, 1993.

Hoodfar, H. *Between Marriage and the Market: Intimate Politics and Survival in Cairo*. Berkeley, CA: University of California Press, 1988.

Horneman, F. *The Journal of Horneman's Travels from Cairo to Mourzouk: The Capital of Fezzan in Africa in the years 1797–8*. London and Weimar: W. Bulner and Co., 1802.

al-Jadir, Saad. *Arab and Islamic Silver*. London: Stacey International, 1981.

Jereb, J.F. *Arts and Crafts of Morocco*. London: Thames and Hudson, 1995.

Lane, E.W. *An Account of the Manners and Customs of the Modern Egyptians*. 2 vols. London: Ward, Locke and Co., 1890.

Loughran, Kristyne. *Art from the Forge*. Washington, DC: National Museum of African Art, 1995.

Loughran, K., and C. Becker. *Desert Jewels: North African Jewelry and Photography from the Xavier Guerrand-Hermes Collection*. New York: Museum for African Art, 2009.

Loughran, K., and J. Mack. *Ethnic Jewelry*. London: British Museum Press, 1988.

Lynch, P.D. and H. Fahmy. *Craftswomen in Kerdassa, Egypt*. Geneva: International Labour Office, 1984.

Malim, Fathi. *Oasis: Siwa from the Inside: Traditions, Customs and Magic*. Egypt: Al Katan, 2001.

———. *Secrets of the Oasis: Siwan Cuisine and Recipes*. Egypt: Al Salam, 2007.

Manniche, Lise. *An Ancient Egyptian Herbal*. London: The British Museum Press, 2006.

Morton, H.V. *Through the Lands of the Bible*. London: Methuen, 1938.

Paine, S. *Embroidered Textiles: Traditional Patterns from Five Continents*. London: Thames and Hudson, 1990.

Philips, C. *Jewelry: From Antiquity to the Present*. London: Thames and Hudson, 1996.

Picton, J., and J. Mack. *African Textiles*. London: British Museum Publications, 1989.

Reswick, I. *Traditional Textiles of Tunisia*. Los Angeles, CA: Craft and Folk Art Musum, 1985.

Rohlfs, G. *Three Months in the Libyan Desert*. Cairo: The American University in Cairo Press, 2005.

Ross, H. Colyer. *Bedouin Jewelry in Saudi Arabia*. London: Stacey International, 1978.

Rugh, A.B. *Reveal and Conceal: Dress in Contemporary Egypt*. Cairo: The American University in Cairo Press, 1987.

Rusch, W., and L. Stein. *Siwa und die Aulad Ali*. Berlin: Academie-Verlag, 1988.

Sadat, J. *Woman of Egypt*. London: Hodder and Stoughton, 1987.

Savary, Claude. Egypte, oasis d'Amun-Siwa: Musée d'ethnographie, Genève, 1986. Geneva: Le Musée d'ethnographie, [c1986].

Scarce, Jennifer. *Women's Costume of the Near and Middle East*. London: Unwin Hyman, 1987.

Scheurleer, R.A. Lunsingh. "From Statue to Pendant: Roman Harpocrates Pendants in Gold, Silver and Bronze." In *Ancient Jewelry and Archaeology*, edited by Adriana Calinescu. Bloomington, IN: Indiana University Press, 1996. pp. 152–171.

Schienerl, Peter W. "Spanish/Mexican Dollars in Egypt: Currency—Raw Material for Silversmiths—Ornament—Amulet." *Ornament* 5, no. 3 (1982): 12 14.

———- "Female Jewelry from Siwa Oasis" In *Acta Ethnographica Academiae Scientiarum Hungaricae* 29. Budapest: Akademiai Kiado, 1980. pp. 167–180

Sciama, L.D., and J.B. Eicher, eds. *Beads and Bead Makers: Gender, Material Culture, and Meaning*. Oxford, UK: Berg, 1998.

Seal, C. *Constructing Death: The Sociology of Dying and Bereavement*. Cambridge, UK: Cambridge University Press, 1998.

Shaw, I., and P. Nicholson. *Dictionary of Ancient Egypt*. London: The British Museum Press, 2003.

Sieber, R., and F. Herreman, eds. *Hair in African Art and Culture*. New York: Prestel, 2000.

Sijelmassi, M. *Les Arts Traditionnels au Maroc*. Paris: Art Creation Realisation Edition, 1986.

Simpson, G.E. *The Heart of Libya, the Siwa Oasis, its People, Customs and Sport.* London: H, F, and G, Witherby, 1929.

Spooner, B. "The Evil Eye in the Middle East." In *The Evil Eye,* edited by C. Malony. New York: Columbia University Press, 1976.

Spring, C. *African Arms and Armour.* London: British Museum Press, 1993.

Spring, C. and J. Hudson. *North African Textiles.* London: British Museum Press, 1995.

———. *Silk in Africa.* London: British Museum Press, 2002.

Steindorf, G. *Durch die Lybysche Wuste zur Amonsoase.* Bielfeld and Leipzig: Velhagen and Klasing, 1904.

Stone, C. *The Embroideries of North Africa.* London: Longman, 1985.

Van Gennep, A. *The Rites of Passage.* Chicago: University of Chicago Press, 1960.

Vischer, H. *Across the Sahara from Tripoli to Bornu.* London: Edward Arnold, 1910.

Vivian, C. *The Western Desert of Egypt: An Explorer's Handbook.* Cairo: The American University in Cairo Press, 2000.

Weeks, S. "Silver: Ornaments and Anklets." In *Cairo Today* 4, no. 11 (November 1983).

———. "The Costume and Ornaments of the West Desert Bedouin." In *Cairo Today* 6, no. 9 (September 1985).

Weiner, A.B., and J. Schneider. *Cloth and Human Experience.* London: Random House, 1991.

Weir, S. *Palestinian Costume.* London: British Museum Press, 1989.

Westermarck, E. *Ritual and Belief in Morocco.* London: Macmillan, 1926.

Williams, J. *Money, A History.* London: British Museum Press, 1997.

Online:

Moussa, Muhammad Ibrahim. *www.siwaoasis.com*

Index